A bride
without spot

A bride without spot

Maureen Mataranyika

1st edition

Published by SERVANT BOOKS (www.servantministries.co.uk)

GodsOyster@aol.com

Cover design by Norohasina Harris (www.godsimage.co.uk)

Norohasina is a Freelance artist, painting Prophetic paintings. You can find more of her artwork on her Facebook page God's image or on her website

PRESENTED TO:-

....

....

....

Dedication

This book is dedicated to my beloved mother Sophia Chizuva Mataranyika who went to be with The Lord and left a legacy of dedication and love for God compared to none. She made God real in our lives and His Presence in our home real. We grew up with God as part of our family, He was a silent listener to our every conversation; He watched every move and rescued us from every trial. My mum did not teach us to pray but we watched her pray every day. We were not taught to give but we watched her give and serve servants of God. She raised all six of us to live for God and make an impact in our generation.

I also dedicate this book to my beloved siblings who are serving God with passion. My sister Adelaide Mhunduru, pastor of Full Gospel Church Mkoba Gweru in Zimbabwe whose life became a role model and inspiration to me and my other siblings. To my brother, Pastor Martin Gift Mataranyika, pastor in the Apostolic Faith Mission Church, Namibia. To my sister Rennie Mkomana Mataranyika, a wonderful deacon in the Apostolic Faith Church, Buhera who took a unique role in our family sacrificing her education so she could work alongside my mum in the family business to raise money for all siblings so we could have a good education. To you all, I say thank you.

To my younger sister, Pastor Maud Mataranyika Masungo who is still in bible college pursuing theological studies and my young brother pastor William Mataranyika the priest of our family

I also dedicate this book to very special people in my life Reverend Jeffreys Urayai Mvenge, my brother who became my father by raising me and looking after me giving me a chance in life; from him and his wonderful wife I learnt a lot about staying focused in serving God.

To my brother Shadreck Mvenge and his wife Mai Alice I will always be grateful. Brother Shadreck saw in me what I did not know about myself; he encouraged me to find God and serve Him with pure motive He was

i

always on my case demanding I lived right if I loved God. This man is promoted into glory but my heart yearns deeply to see my dear brother one day in glory. His humility and selflessness taught me there is a price to be paid if we are to serve God. To my other brother, Arthur Mvenge and Mai Rhoda thank you.

To you my brother George Mvenge and Mai Jackie I love you.

I dedicate this book to my children who make me feel special as a mother. To you Mercy and husband Kaunda to you Maud and Thomas Mabhidhi.To you Anita and Robert Lamb. And to you Pamela and Jonnel Musunga and to you son Timothy Tinodiwa Chikova. And to my grandchildren Maud Phiri, Josiah Jesse Lamb and Anna Lamb.

Dedicated to my friend Laiza Rangarira and to all wonderful members of The Ignite Global Prayer Ministries Greater Grace Assembly. Sibongile Thabane, Ure and Nissi Thabane, Sippy and Dave Mungaraza and Washe and Nashe Mungaraza. Robert and Anita Lamb Josiah and Anna Lamb Tinodiwa, Jonnel Musunga. Mr Mark Fisher and Wendy Fisher, Keighley and Chelsea and Enrico. Memory Nyazika and Grace. Michael and Brian Nyazika. To Patrick Siouku and Kerrian, Somie, Ebuker, Debra and Iffy Siouku to Sister Margaret Chikoore and Joy Tanaka Jumbe. To Dr S Dube and Shaun Dube. To Sister Juliet Martin, a very special vessel dedicated to serving me as I serve God she has been to me a friend, a sister and a great help.

And to my mentors Ken Lurkhurst, Pastor Janet and Bill Findlater and Eurania. To my teachers from whom I have learnt great truths of the word John Shiver, Robin Jegede-Brimson, Pastor Lucy Muzangaza, Pastor S Nyadzo, Kholiwe Chikuri, Apostle Angie NDlalambi.

I dedicate this book to all those who seek a heavenly home.

I dedicate this book to God the Father who sent His son to die for me.

To Jesus the son of the living God who chose to die for me

To the Holy Spirit my special friend without whom this book would not be here.

A bride without spot

Acknowledgements

This book is for those people with an appetite for heaven who see themselves as pilgrims on a journey to an eternal home and are not distracted by the pleasures and trials of this world. I would like to thank all my family for praying for me and encouraging me to put my work into writing. I would like to thank pastor Lucy Muzangaza who has been a huge encouragement for me to go about preaching The Word and to record my work so we can leave something for generations to come. I would like to thank Bishop Moses and Mama Virginia Moses of Overcomers Church who gave me an opportunity to pastor their London Church for three years and gaining more experience which is part of the testimonials in this book. I also want to thank those people who helped me with funding Rita Phiri, Mrs Mudere and Ivy Chiwandire who stood with me in financing the production of this work; to you l say "May The Lord increase you in every area". A big thank you to Sue Wright and Chris White of Swale volunteers services for typesetting this manuscript and spellchecking. A big thank you to Robin for editing and publishing the work. Thank you to Juliet Martin for encouraging me making cups of tea to keep me awake when writing this book.

A bride without spot

Foreword

Three things struck me from the moment that I first met Maureen in a conference we hosted in Whitstable in 2015; her passion for the things of GOD, her love for her saviour and her humility. She is so hungry to see an outpouring in our nation and I have no doubt that she will. Her burden for prayer takes her to meetings all over the UK as she shares her heart for prayer and revival. In this amazing story of her call from her childhood through to the work she is called to in the UK, Maureen shares her heart with us in candour and transparency. Her life is one of being a living sacrifice placed on the altar of service and consecration to her LORD. Her burden for the nation and the purifying of the church are found on every page of this book as she shares her heart. I found it an amazingly easy book to read, dotted with her personal life testimonies. I have no hesitancy in recommending it to every believer hungry to be used by GOD.

Robin Jegede-Brimson
Convenor, Inter Prophetic Alliance
Kent, UK
www.interpropheticalliance.org

A bride without spot

Contents

A bride without spot

Chapter 1
Struggles in the storm

Sometimes we tend to think that when we serve God we have a door that is always open; with easy access, fast, easy and convenient. This is with a mindset that the door to God is wide open for 24 hour access. True in part but if this is the whole picture, why then did Jesus teach us to knock and keep on knocking (Mathew 7:7)

To receive most of the things God desires for us, we will need to fight the good fight of faith.

If we dream of making a dent in the Kingdom of darkness we need to train ourselves to fight through prayer, intercession, giving and more prayer.

We need to have militant faith that is not intimidated by problems, delays or persecution or storms.

Problems are not unique to us. The apostles suffered and some were killed but still held on to faith.

During the time of closed doors, don't spend time speaking words of discouragement, complaints and defeat to yourself.

Pray and find out God's will for your life.

If you are in the will of God, rejoice through the pain and remember it's time to take up your cross and follow the one who never failed.

This pain is not permanent if God is the centre of your life. Don't start a "pity party" and begin to elicit sympathy from people they also have their own issues.

God did not call us to be in that place to breed bitterness in us, but rather through it all that we may learn to trust in him (Mark 6:47-51).

Jesus was far away on the land in a different geographical position from the disciples. They were on the sea, in a boat, they had enjoyed a day of seeing miracles and miraculous multiplication but now they were alone at sea.

Jesus saw them toiling at rowing the boat. It was the 4th watch of the night at between 3am to 6am. Doctors say that's when our blood sugar levels are lowest. That's the time it's hardest to stay awake. At that hard time of the night, the storms tormented them and Jesus saw them from afar. I find that interesting when the struggle is hardest, Jesus sees us and he is not too far. He began to walk towards them as if he would pass them in their toil.

Does that sound familiar? Looks like God is passing by when other ministries are flourishing and you seem like you are not making any progress.

When everyone around you is getting married and it seems you have gone to every dating website and advertised yourself as a seriously desperate female at "helpmefindahusbandnow.com" but it looks like he is passing by.

When they saw him they thought it was a ghost. In that moment when we are at the end of ourselves, we are most likely to attribute all suffering and pain to the devil. They said to themselves it is a ghost, for to the disciples everything seemed to be getting worse and not better in the road of ministry.

Jesus appeared and said, "It is I do not be afraid". We need to ask ourselves what He is teaching us. The disciples knew that He would soon show up even as with us today at the worst storm he promised us never to leave us nor forsake us, He will show up. I have been teaching in church recently and said when I reach rock bottom, He is that rock under my slippery feet giving me stability, and He is the rock on which I stand.

Struggles are part of our journey with him (Luke 22v42). Jesus got to a point where he cried out "Father, if it is your will take this cup away from me, nevertheless not my will but yours be done". Jesus prayed this prayer in Gethsemane; something was just about to happen. A few moments from that prayer He was going back to the Father but it was His darkest moment. The most difficult, a make or break moment. He was born to redeem humanity it is now or never, He is almost too weak to accomplish his assignment at that moment, He turns to the Father. We get to that place in our lives when our best is not good enough, our ability fails and we ask for God's will to be done in our lives and his will is not to harm us or to hurt us but to bring us to an expected end.

We need to get to that place of peace while the battles of life rage on. God has allowed certain things to happen in our life and while we are still here it's not in our place to ask why. For, one day in glory we shall understand why He allowed us to pass through rejection, persecution, abuse, lack, singlehood and all those situations that caused us to cry out.

In all these sufferings a great blessing awaits us. Imagine Jesus in Gethsemane with a reunion with the Father awaiting Him and if He had chosen the easy way out to call ten thousand angels to make war with the demonic forces and the Roman army and Jewish people crucifying Him, He would have won no doubt but redemption for humanity would have been lost that same day.

The decision He made has affected not just you and me but generations to come and when one day we see Him in his full glory we shall rejoice at such suffering that bought us life.

When we are facing storms of life it is not easy to trust in his faithfulness. It is much easier to believe the devil is in charge and can do anything he wants with us but the disciples were comforted "fear not it is I" (Mark 6 :47-51). They thought it was a ghost.

On 28th September 2015, The Lord encouraged me while I was facing severe financial attack, at that moment it was a ghost I saw and the storm was at its worst, I was almost drowning in debt. The bailiffs were knocking on the door every day threatening to take furniture from the house. The council was taking me to court for non-payment of council tax. Southern water was making threats, the gas and electric companies changed me to "pay as you go". Nothing was working at all. I was running an itinerant ministry and had no source of income during this time. I made a decision to draw closer to The Lord despite The Storm. I would set aside time to seek his face in prayer sometimes alone in quiet solitary places. The Saint Mary's Abbey became a regular place for me and this gave me an opportunity to be silent and hear what The Lord had in store for me. I knew I could not resolve any of my problems apart from prayer. Then these profound revelations were made to me. The enemy would not torment me financially if I were no value to God. It was not an evil man that was troubled in the bible but a righteous man. (Job 2:3)

We learn that in serving God, we anger the enemy and he will not allow us to gain ground spiritually. He who commits his life to prayer is a prime target.

I may never know why certain experiences come but I know his hand moves with infinite love and he is creating intricate beauty in me. Adversity is not a bad thing, in the end I learn to trust him more (Psalms 89:20-27)

v20 – I have found my servant, David, with my Holy oil I have anointed him

v21 – With whom my hand will be established. Also my arm shall strengthen him

v22 – The enemy shall not outwit him, nor shall the son of wickedness afflict him

v23 – I will beat down his foes before his face and plague those who hate him

v24 – My faithfulness and my mercy shall be with him. And in my name shall his horn be exalted

v25 – Also I will set his hand over the sea. And his right hand over rivers v26 – He shall cry to me "you are my father, my God and the rock of my salvation

v27 – Also I will make him my firstborn. The highest of the Kings of the Earth

David's relationship with God was characterised with intimacy. In the storms of life we cry out "My Father". It's these times that makes us grow more in love with him as we go through trials most people walk away from God and become defiant of his dealings with us but these are times that we see from scripture, David solely relying upon God. These verses refer to a messianic picture where Jesus always talked about his Father. David is a type of Christ and this is our hope as well, to find a relationship with our heavenly father especially when we are in a storm.

Many people recoil when they are in situations and begin to ask questions like, "Why me?" Why is God allowing this to happen to me? If He loves me why is he silent? But can clay talk to the potter and say, "What are you doing?" He is the potter and we are the clay. Let him shape you and mould you and train you and strengthen you. His plan is to bless you so that you can be a blessing to others.

When children are woken up in winter to go to school, they think they are doing the parents a favour but when they became chief executives in great places they remember it was good they went through that training. Our Father is a great trainer. Every place he allows us to go through, he knows it is for our own good.

Storms are going to be a great part of our lives as long as we live in this world and are living for God. Someone once said "Don't worry about the bad times or the good times because neither of them are going to last". We need to make up our minds that whatever happens outside stays outside and does not affect what's inside. Don't let the bills affect the peace of the heart. The Bible says, "He keeps in perfect peace whose mind is stayed on thee". What it means is the trouble and the storms can rage on outside but inside, keep in tune, sing melodies in your heart, worship him in those darkest moments when the world outside is not making sense. When the divorce papers are being served and when your son has been sent to the young offenders prison; sing praises to Jesus when there is no money in your purse and you put your card in the ATM and the message pops up "are you crazy don't you know you are overdrawn."

When the car is impounded and you cannot make sense of the world – When your loan application is rejected sing praises.

Let me encourage someone here, when the engagement is broken and when your name is all over social media and everyone is making a joke of your circumstances - worship Jesus.

When you have failed and cannot make your grades and they expel you for poor performance just sing praises and let your heart connect to the Father.

Many years ago, a man named George Matheson was told by his doctor that he was going blind. He pursued his studies and graduated at Glasgow University in 1861 at the age of 19. By the time he finished, he had lost his sight. To make matters worse, his fiancée returned the engagement ring with a note; it read "I cannot go through life bound by the chains of marriage to a blind man". Matheson never married and never fully recovered from his broken heart. He became a powerful pastor yet occasionally, the pain of loneliness flared up, as it did later at his sister's wedding. The ceremony brought back memories of the love he had lost. In response he turned to the incredible love for God for comfort and wrote these words on June 6th 1882,

"O love that will not let me go, I rest my weary soul in thee: I give thee back the life I owe, that in thine ocean depth its flow may richer, fuller be"

It's not easy but it has been done and yes, we can do this in those trying times.

Remember God loves you with incredible love, he is not letting us down, and He is giving us an invitation to cry out Father in the heaviest storms of our lives.

The things we see outside are temporary, they are subject to change – they are not permanent, not real but the things we cannot see which is God's word and the promises they are eternal, governing the things we see. Trust Him and trust His word. He who called us is faithful. He promised us that He will never leave us nor forsake us.

Struggles in the storm

CHAPTER 2

The assignment

A call to duty

A bride without spot

How do you know God has called you? This is always associated to your gifts.

We cannot assign ourselves to do Gods work but we can pray to find out what God wants to do with our lives. Imagine if you create an aeroplane only to put the wrong fuel in or the wrong tyres, or ask a bus driver to fly it, there will be chaos.

Many people take time to study for a trade, some take three years. Doctors take six years; Pilots take three years before they can begin to operate in a professional position. The church has a serious problem today. While in the world we cannot allow a two-year-old child to fly us on a plane or to drive a bus. We have seen a lot of babies try to run ministries, how does that work? Some may argue and say Samuel heard God when he was only eight, that is very true but he was already under instruction at that early stage of life from a man of God, Eli. He was in the temple observing the ways of the temple and learning until he heard a voice. Even when he had heard that voice he went to check with the man of God in the house at that time.

An assignment is from God. It means you go to report to the one who assigned you in the first place. God can assign anyone to serve him, male or female; even animals. In the bible we see a donkey assigned to rebuke a greedy prophet. A dove sent out to check if the earth was dry after the flood. God is God; He is the one who qualifies those He has assigned when God has called us, we honour Him with our obedience.

God has a specific assignment for each one of us; it is up to us to find out what that is. He has laid down a road map for all of our lives and has given us The Holy Spirit to help us find out that God given assignment. We need to seek Him in prayer, in fasting and meditating on his word.

God will reveal His purposes for our lives through His Holy Word. We need to read and study the scriptures prayerfully so we can find out His will for us. The Holy Spirit will help us make the right decisions based upon the word of God. We are called first and foremost to have fellowship with God and to press into the things of God. God needs my hand in bringing nations to Him but He cannot go against our will.

He gave every person a right to choose (Deuteronomy 30:15) "See I have set before you today life and good, death and evil".

Our wills belong to us, even Satan cannot use you against your will; it's totally given to us.

Jesus cried out "Father, if it is your will, take this away from me: Nevertheless not my will, but yours, be done" (Luke 22:42) He said this because we are masters of our will so we must make a choice to surrender that will to God otherwise we are on a self-destructive path to a lost eternity – hell. A question I have always asked myself for many years was – where was the first sin committed? I realized that many people believe that it was in the garden where Adam and Eve ate the fruit and for many years, I believed this until I realized that the first sin was in the Holy of Holies when Lucifer Satan rebelled against God. In that very place where all angels worshipped Holy, Holy, Holy an un-submitted will was willing to exalt itself above God, (Isiah 14:13) "For you have said in your heart, 'I will ascend into heaven, I will exalt my throne above the stars of God, I will sit on the mount of congregation, I will ascend above the heights of the clouds, I will be like the most high' "

Satan was once an angel, one of the archangels called Lucifer. He fell in love with his own beauty which God had given him. He fell into pride because of his God given gifts and assignments. He became self-centred and could not put his will under the will of the one who made him. His rebellion is manifested in the five statements of "I will" addressed against God.

The name Lucifer means son of the morning – light bearer – but the light was turned into darkness. His main sin was unchecked personal ambition – desiring to be equal to God or to be above God, 'I will' occurs 5 times this is self-will that asserts independence from God. The most high God.

We are living in an era where people have lifted their will against God. The bible clearly states we should not kill but many women are comfortable with abortion. The reason for this is the "I will do what I want" despite God. We are living in an era of total independence from God, May our prayers be "Thy kingdom come. Thy will be done".

Jesus cried to Father, "Not my will but yours be done". God is looking for people who will willingly lay their will to the master.

We as the assigned of God should desire to seek Gods will in everything we desire to do. If we are in Gods will, everything that will happen in our lives will be by His permission and His will carries inside it a seed that is intended to be a blessing. Obeying God and living in his will is always good.

Satan was planning rebellion in the same place where other angels were worshipping. Is it a surprise that in the same church, some are blessed and others are cursed? They hear the same words, just like the same sun that hardens clay is the same sun that melts butter. Some, after a preaching, break down in tears and repent of their sins while others harden their hearts and walk out of the church worse than when they came in. If our will is not surrendered to Gods will, we cannot hear God's voice even in the same church where other people are blessed. A parent knows if you reprimand children, one can come and breakdown in tears asking for forgiveness while another would stand in defiance and get into a fight with you. What is happening here is one's will is yielded to the Holy Spirit whilst the other is a rebellious spirit.

There is a psalmist who sang,

Change my heart oh God,

Make it ever true,

Change my heart oh God,

May I be like you.

15

A bride without spot

You are the potter,

I am the clay,

Make me and mould me,

This is what I pray,

Change my heart oh God,

Make it ever true,

Change my heart oh God,

May I be like you.

Today we have a lot of men and women of God who have fallen in love with the gifts God has given them and are using those to their own advantage. I have never seen a mango tree produce mangoes and eat them but it does so other can benefit. A will surrendered to God will always serve for God's glory. You know that you are doing your God given assignment when you go to the one who called you to report. Jesus often separated himself so that he could be alone praying to Him. He went into the wilderness to pray and fast, seeking a close contact with the one who sent Him. What we see happening on Calvary was the graduation ceremony of a life lived under the will of God. Jesus shed his blood, the atoning blood that would be taken to the Holy of Holies in heaven to cleanse the first place where sin was committed, the first sin that Jesus dealt with and got eternal victory through His blood. Now we are all redeemed by that precious blood we cannot give God any sacrifice. Nothing is higher or better than The Blood but we can do something, we can give Him our will and say,

"Let your kingdom come in my heart and let your will not mine be done in my life. Then we take up our cross and serve him"

In following God's given assignment, there are five questions you ask yourself:-

1. Who am I?
2. Where did I come from?
3. What is my purpose on earth?
4. How do I conduct myself? Issues of morality and Holiness
5. Where am I going to when I die? Heaven or Hell?

If you can answer the first question then the rest is easy.

Our Father does not want us to sin. There are certain benefits that go with being called of God. Each person God gives an assignment He surrounds with favour, grace, mercy, provision and test. You cannot write the same test even if you are called as a couple. Each one has their own test paper.

Once God has called you, He gives you reassurance that you will always come out no matter what the trial is. He empowers you for the journey if you keep your eyes on him. He promised us "all authority" (Mathew 28:18) if we are serving him. We are called to teach the world about salvation and teach people to walk with the Lord for themselves and not make us (leaders) their idols. Pray for those God has given gifts to serve.

Jesus is our friend but He is Holy and is looking at our hearts. He wants us filled with living water. We teach wives to be honouring to their husbands and husbands to treat their wives like a treasure, children to honour parents. Moses built a portable temple and Solomon built a solid temple but Jesus wants us to be His temple keeping in line with his word and getting guidance from The Holy Spirit for day to day living. Developing a habit of studying His word everyday lest we slip. If we slip a little we may end up losing something priceless.

God gave Adam a blessing (Genesis 1:27,28. God created man in His own image; in the image of God He created them male and female. Then God blessed them and God said to them, "Be fruitful and multiply, fill the earth and subdue it – have dominion over the fish of the sea". We are image bearers on this earth and it therefore follows that we are blessed.

There is an inborn capacity in all of humanity to succeed – God wants us to focus on what's important. He has not called us to be impoverished. He says, "Trust Me". As we focus on God. His blessing follows us.

When we choose to do what God has assigned us to do and walk in His will we will offend many people. Our relationship with God must grow from glory to glory and what happens in the closet will begin to affect our environment. Some people have served God driven by greed but Jesus must be the Captain of the vessel of our ship and our eyes should be on Him and our eternal reward rather than the immediate blessing.

- As we live a blessed life we need to grow in love and sharing our resources with those less privileged and always put God first on our priority list

- We are called to serve one another and love one another

- In serving God we realise we are called to walk with others

- God has given us capacity to love – to create wealth to serve Him. Capacity and ability constitutes accountability and responsibility. We should never be satisfied in just existing without asking God why He created us and finding that out so we can reach our highest potential. To do less is to be unfaithful stewards.

Chapter 3

Jesus is coming soon!
Are you ready?

We have heard many preachers proclaim the second coming of The Lord Jesus. The question to ask and answer is: Are we ready? Is the church preaching His coming? Are we ready for Him? Our state of preparedness will attract Him to come.

Ephesians 5:27 "that He might present her to Himself a glorious church, not having spot or wrinkle or any such thing, but should he holy and without blemish". This scripture sheds light on the kind of preparedness compared to that of an earthly bride.

In preparing for a wedding the bride goes to great lengths in preparation for the wonderful day incurring enormous expenses just in preparation for one day. This takes shedding of weight in order to fit into the right size and look right on the day; a lot of sleepless nights in preparation, exercises, dance practice, acquiring necessary accessories etc just for one day.

If on the day of wedding the bride appears with brown sauce and tomato sauce on the dress it becomes a shame not only to the bride but family and loved ones, so this is a day of great importance – presentation is everything for both family and friends, everyone expects the bride to wow the audience.

Jesus is coming for a church which is His bride that has not defiled its garment with the sins of this world. No one knows when Jesus is coming but Jesus has predicted the events that will take place before He comes.

Matthew 24 from verse 3.
4 - And Jesus answered "Take heed that no one deceives you
5 - For many will come in my name saying, 'I am Christ' and will deceive many
6 - You will hear of wars and rumours of war ….
11 - And many false prophets will rise up to deceive many
12 – Lawlessness will increase and this gospel of the Kingdom will be preached in all the world as a witness to all nations, and then the end will come. The love of many will grow cold.
13 – But He who endures to the end will be saved".

And more warnings in verses 30 – 31 and Mark 13

These warnings are meant to prepare us of this coming. The devil is very busy at the moment, deceiving many Christians with a gospel that leads them to hell. Today churches fill up with people who want to hear funny stuff, prosperity gospel, success and motivational speaking. I have heard of a big church on their end of year night prayer meeting they invited a comedian to entertain the church. When we see these things we must be warned – Is this a preparation for the soon coming King or are we just playing religious games? My advice is if you find yourself in a church like this run for your life find a place where people are passionate about serving God in spirit and in truth.

Rev 20:12 says "and I saw the dead, great and small standing before the throne and books were opened. Another book was opened, which is the book of life. The dead were judged according to what they had done as recorded in the book".

I encourage you, my friend, to take these scriptures seriously and if you know anything would hinder you from meeting with The Lord then prepare yourself through repentance. Repent of all the things that you know do not please God. Give your life to Christ before it's too late and dedicate yourself to serving Him, for a day will come when we shall all stand before the judgement seat of God, each one answering for what they have done while in this body. On that day, your mother or father will not speak for you, your friends and colleagues will not say anything in your defence – there is no lawyer to defend you. It is a dreadful thing to fall into the hands of The Mighty God. In my culture, they have an adage that says in literal translation, "There is no prayer beyond the grave". No one can pray you into heaven on that day. The choices we make today and the way we choose to live our lives will determine whether we make heaven or hell on the day of judgement.

Jesus came as a baby and lived as a carpenter, but guess what He is not a baby nor a carpenter but The King of Kings and Lord of Lords. When He comes again He is not going into a manger but He comes with great power to judge the world so I beg you to repent before it's too late.

21

(Ecclesiastes 12:13-14) When we repent we choose to live our lives for Him. Everything we do goes on record, good or bad. We remember to love our neighbour as ourselves doing good to all people, visiting the sick, those in prison and sharing our resources with the less privileged. We also are called to share our faith with the lost.

We have a serious problem today because we are comfortable to discuss Jesus as a historical figure who lived in Israel, we even make trips to see where He was born and see all the physical places He walked but we fail to realise He is alive, He has not lost His relevance. We are tied up with worldly activities and we fail to realise He is coming soon. Time is up and the church is sleeping.

The church has lost its appetite for the true word of God and has entangled itself with the love of this world (Mark 4:19). The cares of this world are choking the church out of its love for Jesus. People feel that material possessions is a sign of God's blessings but due to these cares many Christians have lost their values and are caught in a trap doing everything the world does just to acquire material possessions. Churches get emptier on Sundays because people want to work so that they can show off to others their latest material acquisitions. They are not sensitive to the heavenly sirens blowing – get ready church Jesus is coming.

1968 PROPHECY BY 90-YEAR-OLD WOMAN IN NORWAY.

Whenever I am asked to come and preach I feel a heavy burden to prepare people of the soon coming King. Jesus is coming for a church that has no spot or wrinkle. He is coming soon as a groom for His bride but as the bride of Christ are we ready? Many people try to speculate and even try to put dates as to when Christ will come but it's not biblical. No one knows the day or the time of His coming all we know are the events that will take place as recorded in the book of Matthew 24. I also believe God has continued to speak to His servants in the past and present to encourage people to be ready for His coming and the following prophecy sits very well in my spirit and I am comfortable to share it wherever I go preaching.

1968 PROPHECY

An old woman of 90 from Valdres in Norway had a vision from God in 1968. Evangelist Emmanuel Minos had meetings where she lived. He had an opportunity to meet her and she told him what she had seen. He wrote it down, but thought it to be so unintelligible that he put it in a drawer. Now 40 years later, he understands he has to share the vision with others. The woman from Valdres was a very alert, reliable, awake and credible Christian, with a good reputation among all who knew her. This is what she saw:

"I saw the time just before the coming of Jesus and the outbreak of the third World War. I saw the world like a kind of globe and saw Europe, land by land. I saw Scandinavia. I saw Norway. I saw certain things that would take place just before the return of Jesus, and just the last calamity happens. A calamity the likes of which we have never experienced.

She mentioned four waves:
1 -"First before Jesus comes back and before the third World War breaks out there will be a 'détente' like we have never had before. There will be peace between the super powers in the east and the west, and there will be a long peace (remember that it is in 1968 when the cold war was at its highest - E. Minos) in this period of peace there will be a disarmament in many countries, also in Norway and we are not prepared when it (war) comes. The third World War will begin in a way no one would have anticipated and from and unexpected place

2. A lukewarmness

A lukewarmness without parallel will take hold of the Christians, a falling away from the Christianity living. Christians will not be open to penetrating preaching. They will not, like earlier times, want to hear of sin and grace, law and gospel, repentance and restoration. There will come a substitute instead: prosperity (happiness) Christianity. The important thing will be to have success, to be something: to have material things, things God never promised us this way. Churches and prayer houses will become emptier and emptier. Instead of the preaching we have been used to for generations – like, to take up your cross and follow Jesus – entertainment, art and culture will invade the churches where there should have been gatherings for repentance and revival. This will increase markedly just before the return of Jesus

3. Moral disintegration

There will be a moral disintegration that old Norway has ever experienced the likes of. People will live together like married without being married. (I do not believe the concept of co-habiting existed in 1968 E. Minos) much uncleanness before marriage and much infidelity in marriage will be natural (the common) and it will be justified from every angle. It will even enter Christian circles and we put it – even sin against nature. Just before Jesus comes there will be TV programmes like we have never experienced. (TV had just arrived in Norway in 1968. E. Minos)
TV will be filled with such horrible violence that it teaches people to murder and destroy each other and it will be unsafe on our streets. People will copy what they see. There will not be only one station on TV; it will be filled with many 'stations'. (She did not know the word 'channel' which we use today. Therefore she called them stations. E. Minos). TV will just be like the radio where we have many stations and it will be filled with violence. People will use it for entertainment. We will see terrible scenes of murder and destruction one after the other and this will spread in society. Sex scenes will also be shown on the screen, the most intimate things that take place in marriage". (I protested and said we have a paragraph that forbids this kind of thing. E. Minos) There the old woman said: "It will happen and you will see it. All we have had before will be broken down and the most indecent things will pass before our eyes."

4. Immigration

People from poor countries will stream to Europe. (In 1968 there was no such thing as immigration. E. Minos) They will also come to Scandinavia

– and Norway. There will be so many of them that people will begin to dislike them and become hard with them. They will be treated like the Jews before the Second World War then the full measure of our sins will have been reached. (I protested at the issue of immigration. I did not understand it at that time - E.Minos).

The tears streamed from the old woman's eyes down her cheeks. "I will not see it but you will. Then suddenly Jesus will come and the third World War breaks out. It will be a short war." (She saw it in the vision)

All that I have seen of war before is only child's play compared to this one and it will be ended with a nuclear bomb. The air will be so polluted that one cannot draw one's breath. It will cover several continents – America, Japan, Australia and the wealthy nations. The water will be ruined (contaminated). We can no longer till the land. The result will be that only a remnant will remain. The remnant in the wealthy countries will try to flee to poor countries but they will be as hard on them as we were on them.

I am so glad that I will not see it but when the time draws near you must take courage and tell this. I have received it from God and nothing of it goes against what the bible tells.

The one who has his sin forgiven and has Jesus as Saviour and Lord is safe."

A SECOND PROPHECY: WHEN OIL FLOWS

An elder in the Pentecostal Church at Moss, Norway, Martin Anderson heard the following prophecy in 1937 in Moss:

"When oil comes out of the North Sea and along the Norwegian coast things will begin to happen and the return of Jesus is approaching." When these words had been proclaimed people stood up in the congregation and asked the man to sit down and not to speak such nonsense. In 1937 it was indeed nonsense to talk about oil being pumped along the Norwegian coast. Today all the world's big oil companies are pumping oil along the coast of Norway. Norway is the world's second greatest exporter of oil – after Saudi Arabia.

The sum of it all is: Jesus is coming soon (suddenly).

The earth has been in existence for over six thousand years. God spoke to Noah after the flood. (Genesis 8:20-22) "While the earth remains, seedtime and harvest, cold and heat, winter and summer and day and night will not cease". Interesting words to note there are, "While the earth remains", this means the present earth will not remain forever. It has a time limit and if we further look in the word of God we see in 2 Peter 3:10-13,

"But the day of The Lord will come like a thief in the night in which the heavens will pass away with a great noise and the elements will melt with fervent heat; both the earth and the works that are in will be burned up. Therefore, since all these things will be dissolved, what manner of persons ought you to be in holy conduct and godliness, looking for the day of God because of which the elements will melt with fervent heat? Nevertheless we, according to this promise, look for new heavens and a new earth in which right courses dwells"

We are living in the end times. The bible describes it as the end of the ages. The first age was the Adamic Age after the creation and men began to multiply – then another age of the Patriarchs the fathers of faiths who marked a walk with God.

Today we are in the Church age, the last of the ages which will end with a catching away of the saints known as the rapture. This is the age where Christ Himself will descend from heaven with the shout of the archangel and the dead is Christ shall rise. He will catch His Church in the sky and go with them into heaven to celebrate in the presence of the Father.

"But I do not want you to be ignorant, brethren, concerning those who have fallen asleep, lest you sorrow as others who have no hope. For if we believe that Jesus died and rose again, even so God will bring with Him those who sleep in Jesus. For this we say to you by the word of the Lord, that we who are alive *and* remain until the coming of the Lord will by no means precede those who are asleep. For the Lord Himself will descend from heaven with a shout, with the voice of an archangel, and with the trumpet of God. And the dead in Christ will rise first. Then we who are alive *and* remain shall be caught up together with them in the clouds to meet the Lord in the air. And thus we shall always be with the Lord.

1 Thessalonians 4:13-17

"Let not your heart be troubled; you believe in God, believe also in Me. In My Father's house are many mansions; if *it were* not *so,* I would have told you. I go to prepare a place for you. And if I go and prepare a place for you, I will come again and receive you to Myself; that where I am, *there* you may be also. And where I go you know, and the way you know" Thomas said to Him, "Lord, we do not know where You are going, and how can we know the way?" Jesus said to him, "I am the way, the truth, and the life. No one comes to the Father except through Me.

John 14:1-6

We are living in prophetic times. Before Jesus appeared in Israel God sent John the Baptist to prepare for His coming. We see one man with a prophetic mantle evangelizing Israel and declaring His coming. When people saw John they could identify him as one empowered with the spirit of Elijah. In him was boldness to rebuke sins and to point men to the coming Messiah. The political and religious system of that day could not hinder him nor threaten him. His word was sharp and the bible tells us they were cut to the heart and repented. Day in day out multitudes came to him to be baptized in the Jordan River. Tax collectors and soldiers joined the queue to be baptized by John. In this last hour, The Lord has anointed not one, but many prophets in the spirit of Elijah, to make way for the return of the King of Kings and the Lord of Lords. His name is Jesus Christ of Nazareth – The Saviour and redeemer of humanity.

A bride without spot

Chapter 4

The Three Churches

A few years ago The Lord gave me a word about the three churches. In a few words I will try to describe these churches and go back to preparation for The Lord's coming. The Lord said The Three Churches look the same in most ways but one needs discernment to see where they are.

THE FIRST CHURCH

This is a church that Jesus is coming for as people in this church strive to lead a yielded life; they fear God and are repentant of their sins. These make Jesus the centre of their preaching and worship. They are dedicated in all the things of God and their focus is not on man. This church has a genuine love for the lost and is motivated to evangelize the lost. It spends time in prayer to find out God given strategies on reaching out to the lost. When they come together they listen to the Holy Spirit for guidance and are not ruled by manmade programmes. Most of the people in this church preach most by their life style. When people look at them they want to know their God. They walk in humility and are not in competition with one another. They are quick to help the needy. They visit the sick and reach out to the poor and those in prison. Their main target is to be like Jesus. They do not desire applause from men; all their good deeds are for God to see. They live a life separated from the world though they are in the world. Their desire is to know God's word and live by it.

This church of Jesus preaches a gospel that says we are pilgrims on this earth and are preoccupied with heaven and making an impact on the lost.

This kind of church does not identify itself with a uniform or some special attire. But rather, this church like Paul lives in two places; on one hand, busy serving The Lord but on the other expressing a longing to be at home with the Lord. (2Corinthians 5:8)

This church does not gather material clutter but shares with those in need and uses any material advantage for the advancement of the Kingdom.

The church of Jesus is Christ-like. The gospel it preaches is not patterned after this world. It's not a man pleasing gospel. The current danger is that man wants to make God in his image. It's not tolerant to sin and uncompromising when it comes to the standards laid down in the scriptures.

This is a church where everyone feels homesick and that this place is not our home. There is a clear understanding of the person being spirit and has a soul and lives in a body. Everyday members of this church work hard in building and maintaining a relationship with The Lord Jesus through reading and studying the scriptures to feed the spirit man. The church renews its mind and soul through the word of God and puts its body to subjection through prayer and fasting.

This Church obeys the Bible commandment to not love the world but to have a heart that aches for eternity with The Lord.

There is clear hatred of sin and many who fall into it repent and confess, rather than make excuses for sin.

In this Church people are given a hope of meeting with The Lord and spending eternity with Him in a place called heaven; but they are also warned that failing to give up a sinful lifestyle one ends in a place of eternal torment and torture called hell. This place was not created for people but for the devil and his angels who rebelled against God, but men by failing to make Jesus their choice choose that evil place. I am sorry to say this God gave man the ability to choose either good or bad and that decision will decide where one spends eternity. The truth is that Jesus died to save humanity from the bondage of sin but man chose darkness rather than light and the consequence of that choice is eternal separation from God.

We see the first Church that survived the flood. It's not a question of being in the majority but in the place where God wants us. Noah and his three sons, three wives and his wife, making a total of eight people, were saved from destruction from the flood while the rest of that world perished because of the choices they made. The Church of Jesus is God's project and God never fails. The eight made it and multiplied.

The Church of Jesus enjoys His provision and protection. In the time of the exodus God provided manna and quail for His Church moving out of Egypt and protected it from attacks. We see that it was a huge Church but because of sin only two, who come out of Egypt, Caleb and Joshua, made the Promised Land – the rest, due to God's judgement, perished in the wilderness.

This Church holds fast the warnings from the flood and the destruction of Sodom and Gomorrah. This Church is aware of the coming destruction. (2Peter 3:10-13) "But the day of the Lord will come as a thief in the night, in which the heavens will pass away with a great noise and the elements will melt in fervent heat; both the earth and the works that are in it will be burned up. Therefore, since all these things will be dissolved, what manner of persons ought you to be in holy conduct and godliness, looking for and hastening the coming of the day of God, because of which the heavens will be dissolved, being on fire, and the elements will melt with fervent heat? Nevertheless we (His Church) according to His promise look forward for new heavens and a new earth in which righteousness dwells"

In this great darkness, this Church of Jesus will shine.

THE SECOND CHURCH: THE CHURCH OF MAN

If you look at this church merely with the natural eye, you will think it's a Church of Jesus. They gather in a building, sing songs, preach and prophesy but all this is man centred. They may have started out well but the cares of this world and the snares of the evil one entangle them so they lose focus on The Lord Jesus. In this Church man takes centre stage. It is a Church where The Spirit of God is not given space. It's in the state like in the book of judges where "everyone did that which was right in his own eyes". The place of Jesus and The Holy Spirit is taken by the "man of God" in the driving seat - the so called "founder" of that denomination. People go by the rules of the man of God. Many in this Church are not hungry for the pure milk of the word of God. They do not desire to know the scriptures by themselves. They eat up the doctrine of the man of God and are led to walk in error. Joshua 1 V 8 instructs us to know the word for ourselves. This book of the law should never depart out of your mouth. It should be your meditation, day and night, but these focus on what the man of God declares. They are blinded to what they call a revelation from the man of God. God has called all of us to depend on His word. Both the priest and the sheep are to feed directly from the nourishing word of God. Many in this Church elevate the word of the man of God above the scriptures and do not make the word a priority.

Their belief systems are made to conform to the man of God's revelations and known experience. The danger in this Church is "the leader has lost the plot then the whole congregation walks in error and therefore a lost eternity".

Many members in such a manmade Church articulate and mimic the leader. They imitate the way he/she talks and emulates his/her lifestyle. Some, in their commitment, worship even the ground this man walks on. We have seen many people break into physical fights because they pledge allegiance to different men of God.

These so-called men of God put fear in their congregation even going as far as to say that to disobey them is equal to disobeying God.

Some members carry pictures of their so-called leaders and in time of problems take these pictures and use them as mediums of healing whether it works or not. We know if it does it's the result of the spirit of the end times. The spirit that seeks to deceive people.

Many caught in this trap confess the name of their leader more than the name of Jesus. These people are not free to live life the way God wants them to. They check everything with the man of God. They feel obligated to please the man of God and subject their freewill to this man of God even when they are being abused they feel the man of God owns their lives. They build a culture around this man of God and he becomes a God to them. They surrender their money and their possessions for the service to the man of God.

The man of God rules over them and his picture is hung in the church and some hang those pictures in their homes as a sign of submission. They can get to an extent of calling him father, which the bible never teaches. On the contrary the word of God admonishes us not to call anyone father as we have only one in heaven, Matthew 23 V 9 – But do not call anyone on earth your Father for One is your Father, He who is in heaven 10. And do not be called be called Teacher for One is your Teacher, the Christ.

Instead of walking with The Lord Jesus and allowing Him to teach them day by day from His word they are comfortable to have this man of God teach revelations claiming they are from God. If a man of God is genuine he would point the flock to the great Shepherd which is Christ the Saviour and soon coming King, the one supreme God who conquered death, even death on the cross.

In real life if we are asked to look after a child while the family goes to work we do not ask that child to call us father. We know our role is temporary. At the end of the day the real parents will come and the child will recognise them but what this Church has done is pollute one another with doctrines of men to a point where Jesus is not recognised at all in these gatherings.

A friend of mine told me a very sad incident that took place in this particular denomination. People in the leadership take turns to do public prayer and as they finish the prayer they must end in a note that says "in the name of the God of _____ (man of God's name). In a particular instance the leader led the public prayer ending it in Jesus' name. The other leaders took offence and took the microphone from him and prayed a prayer that ends with the name of the founder of that denomination. This everyone was in agreement with and they all said "Amen". When a Church gets to this it is obvious that Christ is not the centre of that Church and everyone speaks about the leader in a way that they get elevated to positions of power. They have forgotten that this world is not our home, we are just passing through, and man pleasers cannot see the Kingdom of Heaven.

If worshippers stand up to sing they spend some time singing the name of their denomination and sometimes their leader when the bible clearly states that God is a jealous God. He will not share His glory with any man.

In this Church, they may give reference to the bible but man of God's printed material is made in an effort to silence the true word of God. This Church markets and sometimes reads literature that has been written by the man of God. Very little emphasis is put on the reading of the bible. Young people are manipulated into accepting man made doctrines that do not transform lives.

If you find yourself in such a Church run for your life and find a bible believing Church and let The Holy Spirit open your eyes as you study the true word of God.

There is so much happening in the Church of man. Many activities take place but not much is said about repentance, living a holy life or taking your cross to follow Christ as directed by the word of God but the activities are centred on fundraising and competition in giving. They see the Church as a business, a place to make money, to be recognised and to rise to powerful positions. The message in this Church is mainly motivational, how to be successful. People do ungodly deals just to have money and to be seen as blessed of God. The people and pastor are not heaven minded but driven by greed and self-ambition. People are promoted to leadership positions because of the wealth they have - nothing to do with The Holy Spirit.

The gospel here is tailor made to suit hidden agendas. Marriages are arranged by the man of God and those closest to the power seats get to have the best partners in that Church. Sin on the power level is covered – no-one is allowed to expose the dirty things that happen around the power seat – but there is a God in heaven who sees all the works of men. There is nothing hidden that will not be exposed on that great and dreadful day of the Lord.

2 Timothy 3:1 says
"But know this, that in the last days perilous times will come.
v2 For men will be lovers of themselves, lovers of money, boasters, proud, blasphemers, disobedient to parents, unthankful, unholy
v3 unloving, unforgiving, slanderers without self-control, brutal, despisers of good
v4 traitors, headstrong, haughty, lovers of pleasure rather than lovers of God
v5 Having a form of godliness but denying its power. And from such people turn away."

Now understand this; Paul was speaking to a congregation. He sees that in the last days there would be congregations like these. Men of God who love money (who have no self-control) all of the list above but at the end he warns from such turn away. If you happen to find yourself in this very worldly Church – run very fast, run for your life and find a place to worship where Jesus is the centre.

Most of these churches look OK. They may sing the same worship songs and pay tithes and feed the poor. Many will introduce business like multilevel marketing inside the Church even gambling and say they want to raise money for the less privileged of society. Someone said the road to hell is paved with good intentions. If all the good that is done in these places do not line up with the word of God then there is no goodness there.

Paul describes a Church that is characterised by all kinds of self-centeredness and unnatural perversions. People will maintain an outward pretence, speaking the Christian vocabulary – "God bless you", "It is well", "We thank God", but refusing the heart of Christ. They reject correction from The Word. They justify sins of adultery and fornication as long as they give money in the Church they can keep their leadership roles. They walk with a dead conscience and refuse the indwelling and overflowing of The Holy Spirit. They refuse to let The Holy Spirit transform their lives. They refuse to let the word of God rule over their lives. The bible is the word of God – God breathed His breath over it – but they refuse to acquaint themselves with the word that has power to transform and change lives.

They come to Church to listen to what they want to hear. They are not ready to receive correction and instruction from the Holy word.

"Nevertheless, the solid foundation of God stands, having this seal; The Lord knows those who are His and let everyone who names the name of Christ depart from iniquity" 2 Timothy 2:19

THE THIRD CHURCH: THE CHURCH OF SATAN

When I talk of this third Church I do not mean a Church with a 666 sign on the door. This could be any gathering of people who claim to be serving God but fall under this category of the third Church. The first Church is one that follows Christ with a heart to please The Lord and serve Him on earth until we make heaven. The second Church is run by men and follows the direction of man and not The Holy Spirit. The Church is the Church of Satan.

"For the time will come when they will not endure sound doctrine but according to their own desires, because they have itching ears, they will heap up for themselves teachers and they will turn their ears away from the truth and be turned aside to fables" 2Timothy 4:3,4

From this we can see no one is deceived except through their own permission. The spirit of the last days is a spirit of deception if it were possible to target the true Church of Jesus. In real life we remind ourselves that we would not trust a two year old child to fly an aeroplane for us or to drive a car or bus for us. Every trade must be learnt and certified before anyone can be responsible for anyone's life. When we walk in hospitals we do not see children performing surgery or even nursing people. How come when we get to the things of the spirit and a church mushrooms from God knows where? The "prophet" claiming they saw visions and therefore now want to shape the destinies of men. They have not sat under anyone else's ministry and anointing to prepare and mould them before they start their own ministries. They just fill stadiums overnight and begin to deceive many. Most of these false prophets claim to have a dubious spiritual father who is even younger than them and they start performing signs and wonders. Their messages are centred on demonic activities casting in and casting out of demons, exposing so called witches when they themselves are operating with witchcraft occultic powers. They use power mediums, water, bangles, stones, chains, thread and call everything anointed. The list of anointed objects is endless. They peddle their anointed charms for money in exchange of a miracle.

The end time is a time when God is releasing prophetic utterances through His servants but the enemy tries to mimic God by releasing hordes of demonic false prophets trying to hijack the true voice of God.

But praise GOD, there are ways in which we can look at the word of God so we can see and recognise the false prophets.

We see that in The Word of God in Micah 3:9-11, her heads judge for a bribe, her priests teach for pay and her prophets divine for money. Yet they lean on the Lord and say "Is not the Lord among us. No harm can come upon us". One way to distinguish a false prophet is that whenever they give a prophetic word they attach money to it; they speak religious language asking you to sow a seed to connect to your breakthrough or your prophetic word to come to pass.

There are even pastors who, when they are invited to come and preach, they name their wage before they go yet the bible teaches us that Jesus said carry no purse, don't worry about the purse just go and share God's word. Authentic anointing is not for sale.

The Age of Simon the sorcerer
Acts 8:9 But there was a certain man called Simon, who previously practised sorcery in the city and astonished the people of Samara claiming he was someone great.
v13 Then Simon himself believed......
v18 and when Simon saw that through the laying on of the apostle's hands the Holy Spirit was given. He offered them money
v19 Saying gives me this power also........
v20 but Peter said "Your money perishes with you".

Simon saw miracles and he used to perform like this before under demonic power – then he saw them speak in tongues at the laying of hands and thought this one will give me serious money never seen before. But Peter rebuked him. Simon had been baptised but not ready to lead anyone as he himself was not ready to serve. The problem we have today is we first see these false prophets in a well-known denomination but then the next day they start their occultist miracles. Instead of rebuking them like Peter did we embrace them and call them spiritual sons then give them a licence to pollute the work of God. If this Simon had lived in this age he would refer to Peter as his spiritual father and then start selling anointed pens, candles, oil etc.

Anointing cannot be bought or sold. The Bible says freely you have received, freely give. Do not let the numbers in prophetic gatherings deceive. It does not mean anything to pull crowds – the devil can empower anyone to pull crowds. Look at all these celebrated superstars. They gather thousands in stadiums and halls that are not proof God is there. Simon's quest to buy the ability to impart the power of the Holy Spirit was his obvious sin but the subtler evil was his desire to use the power of God for his own gain. He was going to use this power to deceive people and plant heresies in them.

John 4:1 says "Beloved do not believe every spirit but test the spirits whether they are God; because many see the word many false prophets have gone into the world" The Church is not to be gullible that they indiscriminately accept the pronouncements of all prophets who <u>claim</u> to be of God, that is, to speak with divine inspiration. A spirit is indeed behind every prophet but it may be a false spirit described as the Spirit of the Antichrist and the spirit of error. There are many occultist and heretic prophets claiming to be spokesmen of God. We must therefore pray for the spirit of discernment.

In 2013 I was invited to come and preach alongside a famous "prophet". I went before The Lord to seek Him in prayer and to know His will concerning this invitation. In my spirit, I felt strongly I was not to go but the intercessors praying with me encouraged me to go. The man of God who had invited me was a well-known preacher who used to attend our Church programmes so I thought he was in The Lord so I honoured his invitation. When I got to the hotel, before the conference, The Lord began to speak to me. He said, "You are going to see something that you have never seen in your life. The level of prophecy where people are told their home address and their birthdates but I want you to know it's not me using this person but a spirit of divination".

I was very disturbed when I got there. The place was packed with people from different towns who had come to hear the word of God. I saw pastors from big and small Churches, worship leaders and familiar and new faces. I was asked to speak first. When I got up I warned people about the time we are living in that these are the last days and the enemy is out there to destroy and deceive the saints. He was doing this by sending false prophets who would contaminate the Church by using divination. I warned that even if they tell you some truths it's still to lead you astray. I warned people that the greatest miracle of all times was the parting of the Red Sea but those people who witnessed this miracle could not make Canaan but perished in the wilderness. Only two, Caleb and Joshua, went in. This is true if we will see miracles today and behind those miracles is a spirit taking people to hell. I did not finish speaking. The host of that conference pulled the microphone out of my hand and castigated me in front of all this huge crowd. I cried to The Lord, who reminded me He had warned me not to come but did my own way. I was repenting before Him in that service while the host was blasting me with foul insults. Then he introduced his prophet. What I saw there I have never seen in my life. This young man, probably in his twenties, started to prophesy people's driver's licence numbers and car number plates. He would tell people the names of their neighbours and people were screaming, "Amen!"

When we left the church, I was just asking The Lord to speak to me and comfort me. He did. He sent three people to speak to me, each one with the same words "Pastor you are a woman of God. Watch, this will go nowhere, this is divination. We have seen this before – hold on to the truth". For me those words were enough to know I was in the minority but with God on my side. The Bible tells us by their fruits you shall see them. We are fruit inspectors. It did not take long for me to see when we went to the hotel I was in an elevator when girls walked in. They were speaking foul language and I asked them where they were heading to. I was not surprised they were the prophet's guests. By the end of that year many things had happened between the prophet and his host. Most of it to do with unworthy, ungodly living.

Deuteronomy 13 talks about following prophets. Prophecy and dreams are normal means for God to use in speaking to His people but these gifts can be contaminated by the devil and abused. True prophets are empowered by God to perform signs and wonders but false prophets can, through demonic power, do the same. When Moses, a true prophet of God, stood before Pharaoh he performed miracles but two false prophets, Jannes and Jambre performed miracles as well. That does not make them mighty men of God. Performing a miracle is not a sign that one walks with God but relationship and submission to God does. If any man seeks to move people's loyalty away from God to himself then that man is a false prophet.

The church of satan is full of miracles and wonders but the only reason this is so is to turn people's hearts from God and then they focus on the miracle worker. Some people have bought bangles, bricks and water and all they do is worship the one who gave them these objects. The name of Jesus is not the source of their breakthrough but the mediums bought with money from the so-called prophets.

These prophets live a life-style that does not glorify God. The bible described Moses as a meek man. His life was marked by humility and selflessness. Jesus came and His will was to submit Himself to the will of the father. He suffered shame and death, even death on the cross, but these false prophets speak swelling words. Claiming to go to heaven and back to earth, living their lives in lies and sin, accumulating wealth and building empires. They see this world as their home and their hope is in their material possessions.

Psalm 10:9, He lies in wait secretly, as a lion in his den. He lies in wait to catch the poor. He catches the poor when he draws him into his net. v10 so he crouches, he lies low that the helpless may fall by his strength v11 He has said in his heart "God has forgotten. He hides His face. He will never see".

The prophet is wrong in assuming that God does not see what they do in secret.

Many people who end up in their nets are people who do not have a relationship with Jesus. They focus on their problems and are always looking for a way out – things that the bible never promised. We are called to walk a narrow path full of thorns. We are called not to focus on the thorns but to the one who wore the crown of thorns on His brow. In this world, we will suffer affliction but we rejoice in hope looking for our redemption which is nigh.

We should not live our lives looking for miracles. The greatest miracle was God as man but we reject Him and chase after demonic signs and wonders.

Matthew 7:22-23
The scariest scripture in the bible, "Many will come to me on that day and say, 'Lord, Lord have we not prophesied in your name, cast out demons and done many wonders in your name' And then I will declare to them I never knew you, depart from Me you who practice lawlessness"

Jesus warns against self-deception. These prophets are deceiving themselves and deceiving the flock. It is possible for a self-elected person to exercise a spectacular ministry using the same bible that will condemn him in the end. They can even use the name of Jesus even if they are not walking in obedience and genuine discipleship.

A bride without spot

Chapter 5

The Lord needs to hear this

There are certain situations that come into our lives to challenge our faith. Why do we as a God-fearing people always flourish in times of persecution? I have come to notice that the greatest cause of apathy in the church is always a lack of adversity. The biggest enemy to spiritual growth is lack of challenges. It is when we are under severe pressure that is when we go back to our first love, when we are under severe attack it's when God's best can be worked in our lives. It therefore means every battle we lose is, by default – by failing to exercise victory already purchased for us on the cross. Jesus won a victory for us on Calvary and every trial must point us to that place of victory. It is a time to carry every burden and place it on Calvary. This is a place where the enemy is defeated.

There is a beautiful story from 2Kings 19:11-13. Hezekiah was threatened by the King of Assyria. Hezekiah's response was to turn whole heartedly to The Lord. He tore his clothes symbolizing grief and his sack made of goat's hair symbolizing despair. Hezekiah in his deep distress was driven to cry out to God. Don't we run from post to pillar looking for human answers and help in times of great grief and despair but in this case the King said to himself "God needs to hear this".

God is the one who when he sees our great despair and need, can give lasting solution and comfort in, my difficult situations I have cried out to God.

When divorce papers have been served, is it not time to let God see them? – spread them out to him. He can read and give lasting solution. In my own life when I was going through serious financial difficulties I have been in that place when I took threats from the bailiffs and had to spread them before God and say, "Lord you need to see this". I have seen God's unseen hand move in my life helping me through payments and on one occasion a company that I owed a huge amount of gas and electricity bills to had to withdraw their threatening letters and got me on the lowest tariffs and on arrangement to pay off at a rate of £1 a month. To me, I

44

have seen these moments as God intervening in my situation but at a "quarter to shame". There has never been that moment when the goods in my house have had to be removed. At the right time, I have seen God's intervention.

In December 2012, as I pastored a church in Dalston Lane London, my treasurer brought to me a letter from the landlord that we needed to pay a huge amount of money and move out of the property by the 31st December 2012. The church had been operating at that building for almost 10 years. We had had a few challenges of members leaving and one of the elders had died. As a church, we were in deep grief over our loss and financially we were struggling. If we were to move to a new building we would need a lot of money for a deposit and also for moving our stuff. The letter had come with an urgent threat to vacate the premises in 14 days. We had no time to sit with the church council to decide what we would do and with me were a handful of dedicated prayer intercessors. We called for an urgent 72-hour prayer meeting where we shut ourselves in this same building and sought the face of The Lord. Our Scripture verses were 2 King's 19:14, 15 and Hezekiah received the letter from the hand of the messengers, and read it, and Hezekiah went up to the house of the Lord, and spread it before the Lord.

v15 Then Hezekiah prayed before the Lord and said, "Oh Lord God of Israel, the one who dwells between the cherubim you are God, you alone, of all the Kingdoms of the earth you have made heaven and earth."

v19 Now therefore save us from his hand.

This physical spreading of letters becomes a prophetic symbol of our faith in the invisible God. The creator of all that is seen and unseen

We prayed for those 72 hours, none of us left the building – there was no eating or talking on the phone, it was a serious, urgent matter to us.

We learnt a very beautiful lesson – that our Lord hears and answers prayers. He reads the decrees made by man and he laughs at all their wicked schemes. He is Elohim the creator and there is no God like him.

After that prayer, we approached the landlord who was ready to apologize to us for writing such a letter and insisted we stayed on our same lease agreement. He had told us the building was on a site that was earmarked for pulling down to make room for housing but up to now this is 2017 the church still meets in the same place. Our God is great.

Some people may be faced with a diagnosis and what the doctor has written is like a death sentence. I pray that they take that letter as a prophetic act and spread it to the God of all writings and his pen of love and grace will write forgiveness and healing over any predictions of the enemy. When Jesus went to the cross, he died for us to win a victory over sin, sickness and death. He exchanged his sinless life for mine. He rewrites destinies of men and there is nothing too hard for him to handle. He is waiting for us to come to him in brokenness and ask for his divine intervention. God is the author of all healing. Gods healing may come through medical intervention or through a miracle but God alone can heal. Healing may be physical, mental, emotional or psychological, any healing is from God. God may choose to take our sickness out of us through doctors but he can choose to use instant miraculous healing or slow step by step emotional healing. One time after praying for a sister who was dying of cancer The Lord spoke to me. He said I choose to take cancer out of a sick person or I can take the sick person out of the cancerous body, either way it's my divine healing. We will talk about death in another chapter but death to some is a way of healing; we cannot question God and how he chooses to heal.

Chapter 6

The Snares of
Success

Trust not in Wealth.

Reading through the Psalms I stumbled upon a very powerful verse - Psalm 49: 6 "Those who trust in their wealth and boast in the multitude of their riches ..

v7 none of them can by any means redeem his brother, nor give God a ransom for him

v8 <u>for the redemption of their soul is costly</u> and it shall cease forever

v9 that he should continue to live eternally and not see the pit"

These scriptures felt like I had seen them for the first time. The first thing to consider after reading these scriptures is to look closely at the way we relate with money and the value we put on the human soul.

What is the value of a human being? I stopped to consider how in my native land a woman can be paid for by a token called the bride prize. Many people, before they can place a bride prize over their bride-to-be, consider education, family background, material possessions, physical beauty and many other abilities are added to the list of considerations for value. Parents sit in the family court to decide how much they receive in terms of money in exchange for their daughter. The expectation is the bride will be able to satisfy the family by being productive in child bearing and home building. Value is mostly the judgement of man yet in every man there is a woman, inside that one man is a child – then children and clans. God made one man Adam and saw in him nations of the world. Out of him was going to come a wife – children and their wives until the whole world was full. If we look at a Mr Sam who may call Maureen his wife but another would call that same woman his daughter yet another their Mum and others one aunt. Let's say Maureen is:

1) A wife
2) A daughter
3) A mum
4) An aunt
5) A cousin
6) A sister
7) A grandma
8) A neighbour
9) A teacher

10) A preacher
11) A friend
12) A writer
13) A pastor
14) A donor
15) A nurse
16) A mentor
17) An advisor
18) A childminder
19) A driver
20) A Zimbabwean
21) A refugee
22) A resident of a country
23) A Christian
24) A niece
25) A granddaughter

This list is inexhaustible yet we try to put a value on a human being. To the kidnapper, the popularity of an individual means more money to demand. These are the values man puts on each other but what is the true value of man? This is what Psalm 49:8 answers – the redemption of their soul is costly. Jesus, in the garden of Gethsemane understood the true value of humanity and asked the Father – if there was any other way to redeem humanity from the pit – let's do it that way. If money can buy salvation let's find a way. But Jesus cried out not My will but yours be done. There seems to be no other way to redeem mankind except to die on the cross. Salvation is costly. The sinless Lamb of God took upon Himself the sin of the world and carried it to the cross of Calvary to pay the highest price no man could pay. He paid a ransom for our soul – paying a debt we could not pay. The shedding of His blood on that cross was claiming a lost humanity back to its God. The greatest blessing man has on this earth is that shed blood that washes away our sin and gives us access to our Holy God, the Father of lights in whom there is no shadow of turning.

Today our pulpits are polluted with messages of success. How to become wealthy and not anything on surrendering to Jesus. Money cannot buy salvation and it's not 'the' sign for God's blessing nor the lack of it a sign of God's displeasure in us. If money is the only sign to prove God's blessing on us then drug dealers and all the fraudsters are highly blessed.

Pastor Erwin Lutzer in his book 'Failure, the back door to success' said "if money is a basis for judging success or failure; it is obvious Jesus Christ was a failure".

There is a lot of greed, covetousness, self-seeking and self-gratification in the body of Christ of this generation.
The Laodiceon Church, rebuked by The Lord Jesus – the Church claims "I am rich and increased in goods and have need of nothing". Revelation 3:14-22 They had everything put in order. Their TV programmes were the best, their auditorium compared to none, all equipment in place and the best technocrats operated their equipment. Their conferences were applauded by men. Each year people flew from all over the world to attend the best conferences in the Laodicean grounds.
They had need for nothing but The Lord Jesus says "I know your works that you are neither cold nor hot … I will vomit you out of My mouth v17 because you say I am rich, have become wealthy and have need for nothing and do not know that you are wretched, miserable, poor, blind and naked".

We need to humble ourselves and cry out to the Lord Jesus to heal our eyes so we can see the true riches of His Mercy and Grace and to see how the devil is using money to pollute the work of God and contaminate those who once served in humility now rising in competition with one another over earthly possessions. The problem we now have is once great servants of God are caught up in mammon worship and have used the pulpit to manipulate followers into satisfying their greed. No man can serve two masters - Matthew 6:24. Jesus points out the fate of the last days that there will be two masters – for either you will hate one and love the other – you cannot serve God and <u>Mammon</u>. This is the only time I see The Lord put Himself and money on the same level. In the hearts of man money occupies the same importance and reverence that God occupies. God does not look at money as the comparison to the Euro, Pound or US Dollar but as His rival. The only thing that directly competes with God for your attention, love, respect, fear and worship is money. Money is an idol. Many lovers of money worship it and cannot tithe. When we hear of idol worship we picture some Hindu Temple far away in India that is full of idols that men and women bow before and worship. In this we are wrong. When preaching I often ask people to take out their purses or wallets then warn them that the thing they are holding is not a mere packet or container but a <u>very unique temple in</u>

which the god of mammon sits. What makes him god is the relationship he has with the owner. When offering time comes you see its worshippers sweating for they cannot give cheerfully. The worshippers of God are at peace parting with it.

The other thing is that whenever God demands our attention or time we decline because of work or money related business. We, by doing this, are showing Him who our real master is. In the Church these days if you ask people to come for prayer so they can receive the power of The Holy Spirit so they can go out and evangelize to the lost, only a few come forward but on altar call for jobs, business opportunity or financial breakthroughs – you see the whole place packed we then see who people are seeking in the Church – a god called mammon to serve him.

Jesus did not die on the cross to make us millionaires. There were millionaires already in the world when Jesus chose to die and pay the price for all humanity. He chose us but we are running away from Him and serving a strange god. In John 15 He says he has called us to bear much fruit. Is it not embarrassing to park four cars outside your house when you have not won one single soul to Christ? It's a shame.

Sometime ago I got to visit a millionaire in their penthouse. I was supposed to be impressed by their art work on the walls although I had no clue who had done them. My eyes went around the room that had supposedly expensive wood as furniture – those things did not appeal to me at all; the cold in that place was also severe. I asked for heating and to my surprise was told it was not winter so the heating could not be turned on. What's the point of all that wealth if we are sitting in such cold? These were my thoughts as the meeting was long and became unbearable – not only was I cold but became hungry but was not expected to stay over lunch so there was nothing for me. It reminded me of Andrew Carnegie who said "millionaires seldom smile" unless they are busy working out how to keep the money

God gives us an understanding in His word of the last days. People will be lovers of money. This is how He views earthly wealth. Luke 6:24 "But woe unto the rich For you have received your consolation"

Timothy 6:9 "But they that will be rich fall into a temptation and a snare, and into many foolish and hurtful lusts which drown men into destruction and perdition"

I know it is easy to quote Deuteronomy 8:18 which says: 'He gives us power to get wealth'. This wealth can be identified as money as well as peace, good health, a sound mind serving God and finally making heaven. It's a problem when we limit wealth to mean just money. Money in itself is not a sin but the love of it or putting it above God is the problem. Money can never make anyone rich. True riches come from a relationship with God and serving Him.

If people are in need of money they pray, fast, ask and harass heaven for the monetary blessing. The pastor or bishop who loses money will get angry and agitated but the same person if they lose their anointing or relationship with God just carry on as usual, as if nothing has happened.

The rich man and Lazarus

The story of the rich man and Lazarus is fascinating. One wonders: can a man go to hell just because he was rich. I may not have an answer but only speculation. Proverbs 18 V 11 says "The rich man's wealth is his strong city and as a high wall is his own conceit". What makes Jesus our high priest is not the amount of money he paid for the position but the obedience to die on the cross is what gave Him the highest position so that at the name of Jesus every knee in heaven and earth will bow and every tongue will confess that Jesus is Lord of Lords, to the glory of The Father. The rich man's sin is his strength and security in money and not God. Our own uncompromising obedience to God is to lay down our lives so God can use us as He wills and that we walk with The Holy Spirit, learning and allowing Him to teach us each day. Jesus walked on this earth with no earthly possessions yet people talk about Him as having an accountant, Judas, and having people cast lots for His inner garment. We do not see where they cast lots for His colt or horse because the one He used for the triumphant entry was a borrowed one. Neither do we see them casting lots for the boats He used for preaching or the house where He held the last supper. No, because there were borrowed, owning nothing but possessing all.

The kind of gospel we present is twisted to suit our own selfish greed and self-ambitions. Yet Hebrews 13 V 5 the bible commands us "Let your conversation be without covetousness and be content with such things as you have. For He has said: I will never leave you nor forsake you".

Jesus taught us to be content but we are restless. Sometimes pastors con people for money from the pulpit, twisting the gospel to suit personal greed. Some prophets scare people if they don't give a certain seed they could lose such and such – marriages are sold for money, children and all blessings which God promised freely you have received, freely give. The bible teaches us to love not the world but these teachers call for called to reign the world. Today the Church ridicules the poor and makes mockery of their efforts and struggles. Recently I watched a post where a man went to the pastor to ask if he could pray for him to get married. The pastor, in mockery, asked how much money the young man had and what level of education he had. This young man had no education and no money so the pastor prayed for God to deliver women from the lazy, poor uneducated man. As many viewed it as a joke I was puzzled and reminded marriage is of God not of the pastor and in the Garden of Eden there were no qualifications required before Adam could quality for a wife. God actually blessed Eve with a mandate to be a helper of Adam. How do you help a man who can name all trees, all animals, rivers and mountains – yet God knew Adam was incomplete. There is an incomplete man waiting for a helper from God but the Church mocks because money has become a god which ever defines who gets married or not. Shame on the Church. Some people have been greatly wounded in Churches because they don't have substance (money) so are disqualified from the marriage list. Only the rich make it to the aisle. Is it not sad that Abraham addressed the rich man in hell as "My Son"? If this rich man was a son of Abraham we can therefore say he was a descendant of Abraham and in this day we could say a son of Abraham through faith. He was therefore a Christian known in the Christian church and in the same pulpit where the pastor preached he would acknowledge the rich son and despise the Lazarus who ended up with no wife and no job. May God help the church to see how we have littered the earth with casualti8es due to our covetousness? The 'son' had privileges of getting closer to the pastor even marrying from the 'royal' family while the Lazarus who is spirit filled with the evidence of speaking in tongues but no 'substance' mammon is cast out to pick breadcrumbs.

Jesus gave the church a mandate. Mark 16:15 "Go into the whole world and preach the gospel to all creatures, .. baptizing them.. and these signs shall follow those who believe"

We are called to plunder hell and populate heaven but we preach for people to come to church and not to Christ – to give their purse and not their heart. We are called to walk in signs that accredit the gospel message. When they believe – an inward reception of Christ we then baptize them – that is an outward testimony of their belief. Today instead of teaching them the teachings of Christ that transform man from being ordinary to extraordinary through the empowerment of The Holy Spirit we focus mainly on the outward appearance and material possessions as proof of God's blessing.

Something to think about!!

James S Hewett says: God did not save us to be a sensation: He saved us to be His servants. God wants us to use our material wealth to win souls for Him. 1Timothy 6:17-19 "Charge them that are rich in this world that they be not high-minded: nor trust in uncertain riches but in the Living God who gives us richly all things to enjoy. That they do good, that they be rich in good works, ready to distribute, willing to communicate, laying up in store for themselves a good foundation against a time to come, that they may lay hold on eternal life"

God expects the rich to call parties for the homeless and the hungry. In this world, we just build sandcastles – the reality is in serving God with all that we have.

We remember what the Bible teaches us on laying up our treasure in heaven where neither moth nor dust will corrupt and where thieves do not break through or steal; For where your treasure is, there will your heart be also.

Think about this: An estimated 80 thousand unsaved souls die every day. This is 3,333 every hour, 55 every minute face the judgement seat of Christ.
When we stand before the Lord what is He going to ask for: The money we made or the souls we saved?

It's not everyone who can go to India to preach the unreached or to Africa but if we make a mandate to use our money for the advancement of the gospel we do well.

The bible calls all of us to go therefore and preach the gospel so we share the gospel with all the people within our reach and use our money to reach those who are out of our reach. We send missionaries and we support servants of God who are in the field.

In the Old Testament people were instructed to leave behind some grain in the fields so the poor widows, orphans and foreigners would glean after them. The story of Lazarus and the rich man describes how the poor man ate crumbs from the table of the rich. It is a pity though that today we cannot even afford to leave crumbs and the poor die at our doorsteps. In our churches when beggars turn up we discourage people to give and our defence is that we believe all beggars are alcoholics and drug addicts. There is no more compassion even inside the church. God is looking at how we are hiding even the crumbs from the poor. We fail to realise that we came with nothing and that whatever we have is God's blessing with the Levite, the orphan, the widow and the foreigner. Each person should make an allowance each month to give generously to the work of God as well as to the poor.

There is a great hypocrisy going on in these last days among the believers. Many claim to give to tele-evangelists who sell their blessings for a price. I am not against giving to genuine ministries that are working hard to make sure the gospels go to nations but I see people market blessings – if you give your seed of eight hundred in the next eight minutes a miracle is coming! Seriously people, we need to open our eyes and see through the theatrics of greedy people. It is necessary to help some ministries that are working hard to win souls. If you attend a local church your tithe should go to your local church and then you can pay offerings to the ministry that is working on outreach. We should also remember to give to the less privileged. Our lives should reflect Christ's nature.

Christ gave us the best gift which money cannot buy. That is the gift of salvation. Corinthians 5 V 15 – "and He died for all, that those who live should no longer live for themselves, but for Him who died for them and rose again".

Jesus is saying: "Look, I gave you My life, your life belongs to Me and all that you have is Mine. I do not want you to have any other master but Me".

God wants to see His will done in our lives and one way to do this is to advance the gospel.

Many people will go on to another extreme where they claim to love the poor more than God Himself. They fall into a trap and end up like Judas. These are those who say all my tithes and offerings will go to the poor and nothing goes to the church. Remember God does nothing on this earth except through the church. Yes, the term church has been abused and many con-men have polluted and defiled God's church all over the world and its imperative for each one to cry out to God and ask where to worship and where to give. Judas, when he saw anointing being poured out on Jesus, he said it was a waste and that the perfume could have been sold and money given to the poor. It's sad today that this Judas spirit operates in the church. Many people oversee church finances but they themselves are not saved from mammon god. Judas was in charge of the church finances. He was good at counting what others brought in and sometimes he would help himself from the offerings. He had no fear of God. He was in the ministry for personal gain. This is a man who walked very close to Jesus, carrying His purse. Who do you trust with your purse? Is it not the one you love and care about? Yes, you got it right. Jesus loved Judas to the point of surrendering His purse to him. So, Judas was the one in charge of bookings. He would decide which mode of transport, either boat or donkey. He would decide the hotel they slept in because he had the money bag. He would also decide the food quality and quantities. This man had a privilege to kiss the door of heaven yet went to hell fire.

When we begin to put the poor above God we are heading on a steep road. We give God His place and the poor their place. We serve God with our substance and we remember to give the less privileged. If we love Him we will keep His Commandments to love God (first) with all our hearts, mind and soul and to love our neighbour just like we love ourselves.

Chapter 7

A warning to leaders, shepherds and prophets.

Many years ago, The Lord showed me how the church leaders have failed Him in that they compromise the word of God and pollute whole congregations by setting up satanic altars. They introduce doctrines that are not biblical because they want to be seen as politically correct. They marry politics and God's work just like Ahab who united with Jezebel, a personification of the spirit of wickedness, and this is the antichrist principality behind political governments. The church has become tolerant to gay marriages and has turned a blind eye to the command of God's voice. They twist the scriptures to suit the world and adhere to new laws that contravene the word of God. The word of God does not change. When people look at the church they want to see Christ but we have filled the church with worldliness and to some point are worse off than those people in the world.

This is a trend of the last days. The bible teaches about when you see the abomination that causes desolation stand in the holy place then you know the end has come. I don't know what the (desolation) abomination that causes desolation is but I can say abomination is something unholy – offensive to God and when we see that standing in the holy place this could mean the church or the altar representing priesthood we can break it down and say: If abominable practices against God are being legalised from the pulpit then we should know the destruction of humanity is at hand. When God was appalled by the sin of Sodom and Gomorrah He destroyed the two sister cities but that which God saw as abominable is today being licensed in church thereby causing God's anger on all men who approve of it.

Malachi 1:6 says "It is you O priests who show contempt for my name". Today some priests and pastors declare that they are gay and that they should marry people who believe are born that way. Are we not all born that way? What is that way? It is the way of sin. All men are born in sin. We all need salvation (for) without which we cannot see The Lord. The truth is all sinners of which I am the worst are born that way – the way of Adam. We all carry on inherent Adamic nature which we all need to deal with on our own. It's practically impossible. We depend upon the shed blood of Jesus which, when we accept Him as our Lord and saviour, He can settle the matter of that way so we may walk upright in His way.

58

The priests comfort people and lie to them that it's OK to live that way. Jeremiah 8:11 says "For they have healed the hurt of the daughters of my people slightly, saying peace, peace; when there is no peace".

Because priests and ordained bishops say there is nothing wrong in same sex relationships and many other things coming up like sex change and transgender people have become confused. They point to the priests and say it must be right because priests approve and even partake of those same sins.

We are ambassadors of a heavenly kingdom. When people look at the church they must see how heaven looks like and feels like but the amount of tolerance and mingling of the holy and unholy has become a stench before our Holy God. We have failed God and His kingdom. An ambassador does not meddle with the politics of his host country. He remembers only to work in the interest of the country he represents and is governed by the principles and laws of his own country. The end time ambassadors have lost all connection with the heavenly duty and are mingling and even transferring loyalty to a foreign kingdom.

Malachi 2:7,8 "For the lips of a priest should keep knowledge, and the people should seek the law from his mouth; For he is the messenger of the Lord of hosts. But you have departed from the way, you have caused many to stumble at the law".

God is saying when people look at pastors who have misrepresented Him they cause many people to fall into sin.

Verse 9 of the same chapter in Malachi talks of exposing all these so called men of God - not all are being condemned but those that cause many to stumble. There is going to be a time where so called great men and women of God will be exposed. Every work of darkness and every unholy action is going to be exposed. At a time before Christ's return God will raise nobodies, who will have a mantel of Elijah. These will speak the truth without fear of the government because they are governed by a heavenly authority. These men will have the spirit of Daniel and not fear the lions. We are soon approaching that day where uncompromising men and women will rise up and take on the undiluted gospel to a famished world.

Some pastors and leaders who are growing their congregations using occultic demonic powers will be exposed. There is a marriage today between the lukewarm church and the government. What was wrong with King Ahab was his tolerance of Jezebel. When we elect so called 'Christian Presidents' we expect them to govern God's people according to the word of God but once in power they become more corrupt than the ungodly leaders and walk in an Ahab spirit. They bring in all defilement and even seek to force the church to adapt to these evil practices. God is the head of the church as well as the governments because all creation belongs to Him. If the church will not rise up to the standard of God then the nations struggle. The Bible says, "If the foundations are destroyed what can the righteous do?" The church is called to uphold governments on its shoulders but if corruption starts in the church what is the hope of the government?

Mammon worship takes centre stage in church, so does adultery. Many sins against nature are rampant in the church today.

There is so much revelation on the word of God but this knowledge is not effective because the shepherds are leading lifestyles that are not compatible with their revelations.

We are soon going to see big scandals in the churches but after that Joel promises:
Joel 2: 28 – "And it shall come to pass afterward that I will pour out my spirit upon all flesh. Your sons and daughters shall prophecy your old men shall dream dreams; your young men shall see visions"

This is a prophecy for the end time. God is about to raise the uncompromising Esthers and Elijahs. People who fear no man but only God. These will pray and preach with great zeal. They will rebuke the works of the compromising church and will carry an anointing for revival and preparation of the bride of Christ. These are the army of God – an end time army that will not bow to god mammon or intimidated by the government bills. God will create platforms for them to speak so the gospel reaches every nation. So that this gospel of the kingdom will be preached in all the earth then the end will come. It's not a success gospel or prosperity, deliverance, miracles but a gospel centred on Christ. Maranatha!!!

A warning to leaders

Chapter 8

Revival

This chapter will cover a lot of aspects related to revival. One thing to always bear in mind is that revival is a work of God but God uses men in the revival. Prayer ignites revival but holiness maintains it. There have been many revivals across generations but the end time revival is like no other ever seen in the history of humanity. In my country, Princess Diana was to visit and many things were put in place in preparation of a visit by a member of the British monarchy. Roads were repaired, bridges fortified, buildings repainted and trees were grown along the way the princess would pass. A lot of clearing of slums destroyed. General cleanliness of the city was maintained to a very high standard. School children were taught how to behave when they met with royalty. They practised dances and songs. All the children, who were to greet the princess, had new uniforms, clean teeth and even shoes for the first time for others because this was a very special event – one that would make a lasting impact on the whole country – so things had to look just right. All this was in preparation of an earthly king.

Jesus is coming!! Is the church preparing for His return? How ready are we? Our readiness will bring Him soon. It is very easy to point out that there are fake pastors, fake prophets and so on but have we ever stopped to think of fake members of fake church goers. I can say that if you are not filled with the power of the Holy Spirit then there is a chance you may fall into the category of carnal Christians. This kind of person cannot tap into the spiritual realm where God wants all of us to be if we are to prepare for the coming of the Lord. Our mandate is to first look at ourselves and ask these essential questions:

1. Are we walking in harmony with The Holy Spirit?
2. Are we filled with the power of The Holy Spirit?
3. Are we transmitters or conduits of God's power to the world? For without Him we cannot do anything.
4. Do we know The Person of The Holy Spirit and do we relate with Him?

It's very easy to talk about God, The Father and Jesus as Lord but what place do we give The Holy Spirit who is part of a Triune God? If we neglect and ignore Him He will not force His way into our lives. We have got to yearn for Him and invite Him to be part of our lives. He waits for that invitation.

Many years ago, I was in a very abusive marriage which caused me to hate my mother-in-law. I had been raised in a Christian Pentecostal Church and considered myself to be a born again Christian. I was baptized in water at the age of fourteen and got married at the age of twenty-seven. Throughout my life, I did good works and even taught Sunday school. I used to see people speaking in tongues but I thought that would mess my make-up. The tears and snot – these I despised. I was a high-school teacher and felt it would not look proper for young people I taught to see me crying and speaking in tongues.

One day I visited a very mature woman in The Lord. I had gone there with the intention of telling her my problems – the violence from my husband and how my mother-in-law was contributing to my pain by not saying anything. The moment I spoke those things she looked at me and shook her head. She said you need a new heart and that God should take away your stony heart. That came as a shock to me as I was the victim and needed her sympathy – it was me who had a heart issue. The woman could clearly see I was a good church woman who had no spiritual and moral transformation. She wanted to show me my heart should be on God.

Ezekiel 11:19 – "Then I will give them one heart, and I will put a new Spirit within them and take the stony heart out of their flesh and give them a heart of flesh" – Further reading Ezekiel 18 V 31.

That's where The Lord had directed me then I wanted to know how I could get this new heart. The old lady invited me to her house. In her big house, she had dedicated a room which she called "the operation theatre room" where people would get their stony hearts on the altar and get hearts of flesh. When I stepped in there were around 20 people from different churches. They would come in that room and pray – some would spend the whole day or if possible sleep over. It felt like a great wind pulled me inside that room. I saw children as young as 5 years speaking in tongues and tears streaming down their cheeks. I saw people lost in worship in tongues – no-one preaching but each person just enjoying the presence of God. I had never experienced anything like this even in my own church which had almost a thousand members. In this theatre room there seemed to be no sense of time – no-one looked at the watch. Some people were lying on the floor like they were dead and others lifted their hands in worship for hours. Then I saw a young girl of about six worshipping God. In my heart I cried "Lord if this is of you I want what is in that girl". Before I finished that prayer I was filled with the power of The Holy Spirit and began to speak in tongues. What happened that day changed my life. I had lived all my life with bitterness, unforgiveness, regrets and murmuring but on this day I felt something lift off me and a new experience – heaven touching earth. No words can describe the joy that came into my heart. I started praying from around nine in the morning to about 5 that evening, everyone was looking for me as I had not told anyone where I was going.

When I came out of the "surgery operation theatre" I felt like a new person. It felt like I was seeing trees for the first time. Everything God created looked beautiful and all the people walking down the street looked beautiful. I used to have an unnatural fear of dogs but that day fear left. I opened the gate and the first person I saw was my mother-in-law with arms stretched. I ran towards her and gave her a big hug, still speaking in tongues. Even if she did not understand what I was saying she appreciated the gesture.

I had a duty to prepare supper for everyone in the family. I did that still speaking in tongues. In my heart, I thought if I stopped it would not come back so I did not want to stop. My in-laws got worried and called my pastor to talk to me. When I got to the phone I greeted my pastor in tongues. This must be up to ten hours of tongue speaking and tears and snot and the joy of The Lord. My pastor began to prophesy. He told me a very unique anointing was upon my life but he also advised me to stop as the family did not quite understand what was happening to me. That day I did not eat – I thought food would take away my new gift. I went to bed still speaking in tongues. I had not realised I had just acquired a new friend – one who would always guide me and walk with me in my journey of faith. He is the one Jesus promised would guide the church into all truths – Oh how we desperately need Him in these last days. The Holy Spirit is the person of The Trinity who dwells in us.

The Holy Spirit is needed in these last days to change hearts and minds of people so they are ready to prepare for the coming revival.

Jeremiah 31:33-34 – "I will put my law within them and on their heart I will write it and I will be their God and they shall be my people".

When we allow Him to work through us we are able to perceive the heavenly mandate upon the end time work. With the help of The Holy Spirit working in us we are directed to pray according to God's heart. We cannot work for The Lord without co-operating with Him through His spirit on our own we are nothing and can do nothing.

Our knowledge of God is not going to bring revival but our relationship will. If all the praying people will practice fellowship with The Holy Spirit then the glory of God will fall on earth. The problem we have had so many years is that when we read the bible we do not doubt the personality of The Lord Jesus Christ yet we fail to engage with The Holy Spirit on personal level.

According to Romans 8:27 "and He that searches the Hearts knows the mind of The Spirit", so The Holy Spirit has a mind.

Ephesians 4:30 – He can be grieved. When we ignore Him He grieves. He teaches, testifies, reproves, guides and speaks.

The Holy Spirit is not just a mere force but a person of The Godhead whose participation in the church and individuals is active today just like in the history of the church. God sent Jesus on earth so man could (experience) see God on earth and He says anyone who sees Me has seen the Father. When Jesus talked to His disciples just before going to Calvary He promised The Comforter to come and take over from Him one just like Him not less in importance but carrying the same divine attributes. He is just like the Father in omnipotence. The Psalmist wrote – "Where can I go from your spirit?" Psalm 139:7 reveals the omnipotence of The Holy Spirit. We also find the apostle in Acts 5:3-4 saying, "How is it that you have lied to The Holy Spirit?..you have not lied to men but to God" The Holy Spirit is eternal and He is God in us yet we have carried on without Him as if we do not need Him. In this end-time we need Him more than ever to teach us, guide us and to work through us in ushering a revival on earth which the world has never seen before.

THIS IS THAT!!!

One of my favourite scriptures in the bible is Joel 2: 28-29 "And it shall come to pass afterward that I will pour out my spirit upon all flesh; and your sons and daughters shall prophesy, and your old men shall dream dreams, your young men shall see visions, And upon my servants and upon the handmaids in those days will I pour out my Spirit".

This old prophecy was partially fulfilled more than two thousand years ago when Jerusalem was under Roman rulers. An ordinary fisherman called Peter addressed a crowd of over three thousand people – "This is that which the prophet Joel prophesied about". This was the beginning of an outpouring of life transforming power into ordinary vessels. Man had lost his place with God in the garden. But on this unique day The Holy Spirit has been poured out without measure, ushering a fantastic new era in human history – God living among men. The un-ordained, unschooled, untamed Peter stood up to declare the beginning of a new day. Even those that saw and heard him knew it was not Peter but an empowerment from above had changed this once illiterate fisherman. He, The One equal to God The Father and The Son yet living in us caused Peter to rise up with boldness. He, The Spirit of truth enables ordinary men to accomplish extra-ordinary things.

Once the church can give Him His place then we are on our way to victory. The Holy Spirit was there at creation and when the first church moved in the wilderness He led them as a pillar of fire at night and as an umbrella – protecting them from heat as a pillar of cloud during the day. Throughout the prophetic age He spoke through all the prophets and some Kings like Cyrus, Pharaoh and David. He makes Himself known to lead men to God. He strengthened Kings as they fought wars. He taught men strategies for battle. He warned armies of danger to come. He speaks to all people of all nations directing them to Jesus. He does nothing by Himself but works on equal platform with Father and our Lord Jesus. He gives us understanding of God's word because He wrote it and reveals the time we are living to prepare a bride for the Lord. He convicts man of sin and righteousness and He is that friend who is closer than a brother.

In the New Testament we see God's promise upon Mary. Luke 1:35 "The Holy Spirit will come upon you". So Mary conceived of The Holy Spirit and when Jesus was baptized by John, He descended like a dove. We now see our Lord Jesus giving a command to His disciples not to leave Jerusalem but wait until they are filled with the power of The Holy Spirit.

Acts 1:8 "But you shall receive power when The Holy Spirit has come upon you and you shall be witnesses in Jerusalem and in all Judea and Samaria and to the end of the earth". This promise is for everyone who believes and is ready to be a vessel for the end time outpouring. I was baptized in the power of The Holy Spirit and my life was completely changed. My desire was only to serve God. I was teaching at a multiracial High School and every break time students would gather in my classroom and I would teach them the word of God. Many were spirit filled and the whole school knew about it. Some staff members went to report my activities to the head teacher and he came to see for himself. Children were filled with the power of The Holy Spirit. The Bible describes Him as a counsellor, even the Spirit of Truth, whom the world cannot receive because it neither sees Him nor knows Him. My struggles started at this school. Many thought I had brainwashed the students and demanded I stopped this activity. Fortunately, a move of God cannot be stopped by men. The persecution increased and more children joined the scripture union until the classroom became too small then we moved to a double classroom and after a few weeks we were in the school hall. We began to pray for those teachers who were misleading the head teacher. Our prayer was that they would know God and be baptised by the same spirit as us. God heard this prayer and one by one teachers, senior teachers and heads of departments gave their hearts to the Lord Jesus and were filled with The Power of The Holy Spirit and were also persecuted the same way they had persecuted me.

Towards the end of that year I was promoted to the country's Curriculum Development Unit. While there by the grace of God I started a prayer group where people from different denominations came at lunch hour to pray and many souls came to The Lord. The prayer group still runs today, 27 years later. This is what the anointing of God does. When we receive The Holy Spirit we receive power to serve The Lord. On our own we can do nothing. The Holy Spirit gives us boldness. Jesus said, "As The Father sent me, so I send you". The purpose of the Holy Spirit is to empower us to do the work of our Master, to take the gospel of our soon coming King to the ends of the world.

We have a warning from scripture not to quench the Holy Spirit. We know the world cannot accept or receive the Holy Spirit but today there is great danger than even the church claiming to preach Christ does not know Him nor acknowledge Him. Paul, in Corinthians, warns: Be sure you honour the Holy Spirit. The anointing we despise cannot bless us. Holy Spirit is here to teach us all truth. He wants us to walk in gifts of healing and deliverance. Many people believe this power was just for the apostles on the day of Pentecost but the promise is for us and for as many as God will call. Without Him we are not growing.

ANOTHER ASSIGNMENT

The fire of The Holy Spirit was burning in my heart and after seeking Him I had to leave my job and go into full time Ministry. There was a time that I preached to anyone anywhere - the zeal and passion was great – this could only be the empowerment of The Holy Spirit. In a small town where I went to preach I saw a great move of The Spirit of God. Many people came to give their hearts to The Lord.

EVELYN

A woman by the name Evelyn was brought in a wheelbarrow. Her family had sought help from medical professionals but nothing worked. This woman had children and was married but one day she lost her voice and could not move her hands and legs. The family would wash and dress her and no one could explain this sudden illness. They took her to traditional healers and spiritual churches but nothing worked then one day in the church mission house where I lived I saw this family come to my door. They had heard that a "powerful prophet" was healing people. I came outside and said they had a wrong address. I was not a powerful prophet but just an ordinary Christian preaching Christ. I asked them to go find their 'prophet' elsewhere. One of the leaders praying with me challenged me and said "Pastor, this is an opportunity to make Jesus known". We invited the family in and started to pray. Jesus is faithful; the lady who came in a wheelbarrow came out pushing the wheelbarrow. Many people who saw this came to Christ. Praise The Lord Evelyn is still serving The Lord today. She is one of the elders in the church.

The Holy Spirit empowers us. He works through mere vessels of clay to transmit healing to humanity. Praise The Holy Spirit. He raises the dead.

PRAISE

Walking in town one day I met a couple who belonged to a "spiritual" (syncretic) church – they had a prescription for their one year old son whom they described as dying. I ministered Christ Jesus to them and invited them to come to the mission house for prayer. These two in their moment of despair followed me to the house where we began to pray. We prayed for hours and we saw the child die. I was scared that the police would find me with a dead child in my house so I asked the parents to come with me into the bush. I don't know why I did this but we went to a little forest nearby and we started to cry out to God. We prayed for hours pleading with The Lord to bring to life this only child of this couple. As I held the boy in my arms I heard him cough. Immediately I threw the baby down in shock. Although I prayed I wasn't quite sure of such outcome. I had never experienced anything like that before. The mother picked the child up who started to cry. We brought the baby home, washed him and fed him. Praise The Lord for the work of The Holy Spirit. Today the boy lives, his name is Praise.

SAMUEL

At that same time, the work of God began to grow – we moved to a room at a local school to do our services. There was a young boy of about fifteen called Sam who used to come to the place of worship to disrupt services. He had a small group of boys following him and they would throw stones in the church, laugh at us and just make annoying noises outside the meeting room. One day I got tired of this interference and went outside and called this gang leader. I asked for his name which he gladly gave. He used to call for 'Belinda' a young girl singing in the choir asking her to finish church and come to meet me at such and such. His behaviour was disruptive and very dishonouring. Outside with his gang members laughing at me I pointed at him and said "Samuel, may The Lord arrest you" then walked away. We continued with our service and went home. The next day I heard a knock on my door, a woman crying and asking for me. She asked me to come to her house to see what was happening to her son. I went to find Samuel on the floor groaning, crying and speaking in tongues. The mother did not understand what was going on with her son and thought it had something to do with me. She explained to me that since Samuel had left the church with his friends he had come straight home and went into a room where he had started to cry and groan for the whole night. I told this dear woman that there was nothing wrong with brother Samuel but that he had been filled with the power of The Holy Spirit. Soon after this incident I moved out of this little town and later moved to the United Kingdom. In 2013 I got a phone call from a young pastor calling himself Pastor Samuel. He had been looking for me for many years and wanted to tell me his story. The first thing he said was – "Pastor Maureen do you remember me – I am Pastor Samuel the young man you prayed for many years ago and asked The Lord to arrest me? Let me tell you pastor 'I am still arrested'." He went on to explain the events of his new life in Christ and how he ended up in Malawi leading a great work of God. I got in touch with him and his family and continue to support the work of God in that nation. All glory to The Lord Jesus. The Holy Spirit empowers us to do great work.

Chapter 9

God is looking for a man

God is looking for a man He could own – not partner with but total possession – so He can fix this broken-down church where the glory of God has departed

A man who can pray and touch heaven
A man who can speak with great authority like Elijah
A man who can act in obedience like Noah.
Where is that man who can pay the price for revival like John Wesley, Martin Luther and Smith Wigglesworth?

He is looking for a man who can stand before the religious and declare the coming revival. The present church is in deep slumber but God can work through men and women who are willing to pay the price. Ezekiel 37 – "The hand of The Lord came upon me and brought me out of the Spirit of The Lord and set me down in the midst of the valley – and it was full of bones. 2. Then He caused me to pass by them all around and behold, there were very many in the open valley and indeed they were very dry. 3. And He said to me, son of man, can these bones live?" So I answered "O Lord God, You know". 9. Also He said to me "Prophesy to the breath, prophesy son of man and say to the breath, Thus says The Lord God. Come from the four winds, O breath and breath on those slain that they may live".

This is the breath spoke about in Genesis 2:7. When man was created there was no breath in him until God breathed His breath in man and man became a living being.

This is a calling of God upon the spiritually dead end time church to hear the voice of God. The four winds represent the four quarters of the earth or God's omnipresence. The number four is a sign of completeness or four directions. We can call these East, South, West and North. The breath of God is going to cover the whole earth it's not meant for any one specific location but the whole earth will be filled with the knowledge of the glory of The Lord as the waters cover the sea.

The Ezekiel prophecy may have applied to Israel in that day and the dry bones were symbolizing the house of Israel. Today a lukewarmness compared to none has gripped the church in every part of the world preaching against sin is called "hate speech". It is in a time like this that God is causing His fresh breath to fall upon the four corners of the world. This vision Ezekiel saw relates to spiritual rebirth of the remnant church and this is the same word as Ezekiel 36:26: "I will give you a new heart and put a new spirit within you".

God is calling His church to a place where they can experience Him as individuals through this new birth and new heart.

The work of revival has to start in individual people who are hungry for a fresh encounter with God. These are the individuals God will use to pray and bring heaven on earth. The problem we have right now is a lot of religious people gathering together and calling themselves church. But God is raising a remnant that will embrace the new birth the only way to prepare for our heavenly home where we will all look like the One who died for us. A home where the music never fades and the flowers don't die.

Every believer who awaits the second coming of The Lord must hold on to this tip that Jesus gave before He went back to The Father. Watch therefore: for you know not what hour your Lord comes. Blessed is that servant, whom his Lord when He comes shall find so doing his assignment.

Every man who comes to The Lord has a specific work to do.

OUR MANDATE

As we know not the day and hour our Lord is coming, we therefore focus on our Kingdom Mandate, to preach the gospel of the Kingdom then the end will come. Matthew 24:14 "And this gospel of the Kingdom will be preached in all the world for a witness unto all nations and then the end will come"

This is a very important assignment that the church has been battling with but seems to be losing. The first church preached to thousands with no vehicles and no social media, they were followed by signs and wonders.

Peter and John would say to the lame "silver and gold have we none but what we have we give to you" and true in them was that breath of God and they were conduits of His majestic power calling the lame in the name of Jesus rise up and walk and the lame would walk. Today we can say the same – silver and gold we have none and are not conduits of the dynamics of God. This looks more like a paralysed church with nothing to give but gimmicks. It looks like the ground covered by the apostles is being lost to the enemy through religion. The challenge is for us to fulfil the great commission and maintain it so that revival will come.

For the church to walk in power it has to walk upright before God. The problem we seem to have is that when people come from the world they meet leaders who are more crafty and corrupt than the world and their condition worsens.

Ezekiel 22:24 "son of man say to her, you are a land that is not cleansed or rained on in the day of indignation.
25. The conspiracy of her prophets in her midst is like a roaring lion tearing the prey, they have devoured people, they have taken treasure and precious things, they have made widows in her midst.
26. Her priests (Pastors, Prophets) have violated My law and proffered My Holy things, they have not distinguished between the Holy and unholy nor have they made known the difference between the clean and unclean.
28. Her prophets plastered them with untempered mortar, seeing false visions and divining lies for them saying 'Thus says the Lord God when the Lord has not spoken'.
29. The people of the land have used oppressions, committed robbery and mistreated the poor and needy; and they wrongfully oppress the stranger (refugee, asylum seeker).
30. So I sought for a man among them who would make a wall and stand in the gap before me on behalf of the Lord that I should not destroy it but I found none".

This is a very interesting passage. God was having a discourse with Ezekiel, a priest and a prophet yet He still pointed out there was no man. The problem with the prophetic anointing is that when God announces judgement on a people the prophet gets angry and passes judgement as well. That's just the nature of a true prophet. When Jonah was sent to declare judgement upon the Ninevites he did that with passion and waited to see those sinners perish in their sins. He was disappointed when God withdrew His judgement upon a repentant nation. Today the state of the nation and church is what is described by Ezekiel. Both the government and the church are walking in total disobedience to God's word. The church is called to pray for the government which is equally corrupt. The situation looks hopeless and the prophets see nothing but a destruction of humanity that has rejected God. The heart of God is searching for those who will answer the need, for <u>someone</u> to stand in the gap. The picture is clear, without someone in <u>place</u> in the gap invasion of the darkness occurs and eventually destruction of people takes place. God is placing a special emphasis of a kind of minister above a prophet and a pastor. He is calling men and women to an office of <u>intercession</u>. This is a time when darkness is covering the earth and gross darkness, the people. We need people who will answer the call of The Holy Spirit. It is a call to pray. Prayer will cost time and energy.

Isaiah 64:7 "And there is no-one who calls on your name who stirs himself up to take hold of you. For you have consumed us because of our iniquities" Prior to this statement Isaiah had prayed that God would come down in an earth-shaking manifestation to punish the nations.

There is an interesting interplay of words where God speaks to individuals and then addresses nations. The man of God is seeking one that can stand in the gap for God's people and the nations. This man is one with God. In prayer, he gets an insight into the mind of God and sees the things that grieve God. The Holy Spirit is one who knows the mind of God and as we learn His ways we can be instructed into position to pray according to God's will.

Sometimes when we pray we may not see immediate results, sometimes we may be waiting for many years to see the manifestation of God's promises and God's answers. Sometimes God can bring restoration after our lifetime in another generation. God is calling us to a place of repentance and prayer. He has made it clear from Genesis to Revelation that prayer is the match that lights the fuse to release the explosive power of The Holy Spirit in the affairs of men.

GOD STILL LOOKING

The challenge we have in this end time is that man has already put himself in a box and packaged himself according to his own desires and titled himself. In our streets today we are not short of prophets, pastors, teachers, apostles and these days it's becoming fashionable to add a collar to the many titles coming up – bishop, archbishop, bishop elect and the list goes on. If you add to this list sons of prophets and spiritual fathers and spiritual daughters – the circus goes on without end. It just looks like the devil occupies people with all these mind games so they miss out on the real call of God and the genuine mandate of preaching the gospel to the ends of the world. Instead of invading nations with the gospel of the soon coming king we are caught up in endless celebrations of self-achievement and promotion. It takes a lot of money and time to prepare all these upgrading ceremonies changing titles from pastor to reverend and from reverend to bishop. The world on the other hand is waiting for bread and we are busy taking up titles that God has not even ordained.

We are to be ruthless to ourselves and repent of all known and unknown sin in our lives. We are in this world but not of this world. We move on a spiritual calendar and must be aware of the devil's tricks in this end time. One of which is to keep us busy so that we have no time to pray. We may be distracted by gathering people for one conference after another and have no time to outreach and to pray. Jesus warned us to watch and pray but the world is moving into the church with such force, many are caught in its web.

The biggest challenge we have today is sin. Revival will not happen unless the church goes back to her original place to tackle the problem of sin and openly expose it so men would repent. We must stop making people feel good with sermons that only promise increase and blessings. What will it profit a man to gain the whole world and yet lose his soul in hell. The answer is nothing. Sin has held the world captive for ages and seems not to abate. Revival will not take place unless deep repentance occurs, for the eyes of The Lord cannot behold iniquity. Only righteousness can exalt a nation.

The anticipated end time revival is a spiritual phenomenon which may not be like any other for we have not passed this way before – Joshua 3:46. Many people yearn for revival. Many have read about great revivals in the past and some have experienced some revival. There are a lot of recorded revivals but some may never be read of in print but one day in glory we will find out about them. Right now in China and Korea some people are experiencing mini revivals. Across the world people talk of great moves of God but these are just previews of the great revival that is coming.

A PROPHECY ON REVIVAL BY SMITH WIGGLESWORTH IN 1947

The word and the Spirit
"During the next few decades there will be two distinct moves of The Holy Spirit across the church in Great Britain. The first move will affect every church that is open to receive it and it will be characterised by a restoration of the baptism and the gifts of The Holy Spirit."

"The second move of The Holy Spirit will result in people leaving historic churches and planting new churches."

"In the duration of each of these moves the people who are involved will say: 'This is a great revival'. But the Lord says: 'No, neither is this the great revival but both are steps towards it'."

"When the new church wave is on the wane there will be evidence in the churches of something that has not been seen before: a coming together of those with an emphasis on the word and those with an emphasis on the Spirit. When the word and the Spirit come together there will be the biggest move of The Holy Spirit that the nation, and indeed, the world has ever seen. It will mark the beginning of a revival that will eclipse anything that has been witnessed within these shores, even the Wesleyan and Welsh revivals of former years. The outpouring of God's Spirit will flow over from the United Kingdom to mainland Europe, and from there, will begin a missionary move to the ends of the earth."

Smith Wigglesworth – The way of The Spirit.

This prophecy will be fulfilled and God is looking for men and women who are willing to pay the price.

A GLIMPSE OF REVIVAL

Many years ago, after I had received the baptism of The Holy Spirit with the evidence of speaking in tongues I became an object of scorn in my local Pentecostal church. People called me names like "Miss Fire Fire" or "Miss Holy Holy". Each time we prayed and worshipped it seemed too short for me so the moment worship starts I would begin to pray in my new language until everyone stopped. At times, I would be the only person blubbing and enjoying His presence. I decided to go to church early so I could start praying before anyone came to the church. I met three elderly women who also enjoyed prayer and we would pray together. I also realised these ladies came to the church every day at 6am to pray for the church and the pastor. I joined them and would pray every day for two hours before I went to the school where I taught. Still I felt a hunger for more prayer. I needed to find someone who felt the way I did. I had been born in this denomination and all my family members and relatives were part of this denomination. It felt unrealistic for me to leave this family church; I would be lost without my church and family. I did not know God had other plans with my life.

One day a family member invited me to a new church. I was very sceptical of all these new churches. I used to call them mushroom churches and believed every leader in these churches was a rebel. My cousin insisted I came with her – which I did reluctantly. When I got to that place I was disappointed to see it was not a church. There was no building but a makeshift tent which had no floor but some grass and dust. I was a bit hesitant to get in as I was well dressed in high heels and pretty clothes. Then the choir began to sing. I had never heard that kind of singing – I am not talking of hitting correct notes and chords but the anointing in that worship – pulled me in. Little children were singing with tears on their cheeks. It seemed like there was no sense of time as this one song was sung over and over:

"Then sings my soul
My saviour God to Thee
How great thou art
How great thou art"

And sometimes they sang this chorus in the native language – people were being slain in the Spirit. Everywhere I saw people around me like an invisible hand was gently putting them down. Most of these people were crying out to God to forgive their sins. I looked around determined not to fall down as it would mess up my makeup and pretty clothes. When I joined the singing I was lost in a wonderful presence of God and began to speak with other tongues. Soon I was on the floor. I do not know how long I was down there but it was a long time. The service had started at 9am and now it was almost 4pm that I went home.

I never forgot that experience and each time would think of my church where they would sing ten songs but nothing happened. The following Sunday I went back to my church. While watching the choir sing I prayed that the same anointing and heavy presence of The Lord I had felt in that 'mushroom' church would happen in my beautiful church but nothing happened. The more I prayed the drier I felt. Then the Lord spoke. He said, "This is not worship but worshipalatory". I had never heard a word like that – what does this word mean? Then The Lord said, "These people are not worshipping me but they are worshipping what they are doing. They love what they are doing but their hearts are far from me." Then I prayed why can't you let what happened in that 'mushroom' church happen here? Then The Lord said, "I want you out of here!" - That was hard. How was I going to explain myself to my mum who had prayed for my salvation for years and what of my eldest sister who had preached to me? No way I am not leaving, I thought, but I needed a sign. The next Sunday I went to the funny church and saw the crowd had grown to about a hundred people, miracles were happening and the Presence of God was awesome. The prayer took four to five hours non-stop everyone speaking in tongues, some people on the floor just enjoying God and others crying out in a loud voice "forgive my sins". I gently went on the floor as if an unseen hand was pulling me down. I fell like a feather and just cried myself out. This indeed was a new experience. The meetings in this church were held every day and they needed a home to meet. I had my own home so they asked if they could meet in my house every night. I agreed to that but inside felt I had let down my family who had no idea I had left the family church.

One day the leader of the church came to my house for evening prayers. He started to explain to me how God had called him and how he had started his ministry in another town and that my eldest sister was one of his leaders. I was excited and called my sister who also confirmed what God was doing in her life.

Services were held every day at night, people gathered from 5pm to past midnight and on Fridays people stayed all night. On Saturdays, it would be all day and all night. No-one left the place and many people with all sorts of afflictions were cured. People were healed from cancer, aids, mental illness – this happened every day.

There was so much love among the brethren – all those who had much shared with the ones who had little. Every day people were added to our number. In every town people came to The Lord. In a short time the church had gone to neighbouring countries – preaching an undiluted word of Jesus Christ. People would fast for 40 days and nights on water asking Jesus to cleanse them of their sin.

We were sent to preach the gospel in other towns and villages. We would leave with no money and get to our destinations planting churches and baptising people in the name of Jesus. Many fetish priests and witchdoctors brought their witchcraft for us to burn and they gave their hearts to Jesus.

Officials in government would come to seek Jesus and many gave up their corrupt lifestyles and gave their hearts to Jesus.

True revival will bring many to the saving knowledge of Jesus Christ. The message preached was simple – Give your life to Jesus and prepare for eternity. The message centred on Jesus and the cross as the only way to The Father. I was so pleased to be in this place. My faith was challenged and my walk with Jesus was growing from strength to strength.

If we are going to see revival in England we need to pray and God is the only one who can give revival. I have seen a glimpse yet I wouldn't call it the revival that was just some preparation work. Jesus calls us the salt of the earth. Salt makes an impact – it preserves. God is putting His trust on us to pass on the baton to another generation, one that has not been dedicated to Christ. We are to be salt to this tongue piercing and tattooing generation. The reason the church today is cold is because the intercessors are sleeping. God was talking to Ezekiel and opening His heart for a need for a man who would stand in the gap. The big titles must not forbid us to stand in the prayer place. In this prayer place we are not bringing in our shopping list of material and physical needs but we cry out in repentance, cry out for the lost and ask God for the latter rain.

When we begin to pray for revival we must make a choice to live a holy life.

When revival comes there will be a physical manifestation in the land. Around the time of my new birth a lot of things began to happen. There were lunch hour prayer ministries everywhere in hospitals, prisons and many government buildings. The crime rate came down. Cinema houses were turned into churches. Pubs were closed and churches took over and many youngsters left the streets to serve God.

THY KINGDOM COME

We are living in a very dark age. A satanic age. In most so called Christian countries The Lord's prayer is no longer allowed. A big retail shop refused to distribute cards that have 'Jesus' but can accommodate 'Jihad'. When preaching in public places we are warned not to say Jesus is the only way to the Father. Children dress like freaks and it's called choice. Abortion, which in the eyes of God is an abomination, is called alright. We now live in a very scary world where every sinful behaviour must be tolerated. Very soon paedophiles will claim their own rights and point out they were born that way. We still must embrace whatever the government has legislated lest we are viewed as preaching hate. It is in this world like this that God will raise His end time army that is not tailored to the dictates of men but are willing to walk with God and ignite a revival that has never been seen since the beginning of time. God is calling us to follow His instructions precept upon precept so we can work towards revival.

Preceding revival is a step by step structure that man will follow. Jesus has already done all He had to do by dying on the cross. We need to stand on Christ the solid rock and preach His kingdom. The church is supposed to be the city built on a hill which cannot be hidden. Christ is the hill upon which the church is built. The church is built on the revelation against which the gates of hell will not prevail.

Matthew 16:17 "And Jesus answered and said unto him, Blessed art thou, Simon for flesh and blood has not revealed this to you but my Father who is in heaven
v18 – I say to you, you are Peter (a small rock), and upon this rock (big rock Jesus) I will build my church; and the gates of hell shall not prevail against it"

The church will stand its ground as long as it preaches this revelation without compromise, failure of which it will go into captivity under the worldly forces.

Matthew 5:13 "You are the salt of the earth but if salt has lost its savour, how shall it be salted? It is therefore good for nothing, but to be cast out and trodden under foot by men"

We have a salt covenant with The Lord which we must keep to bring the kingdom on earth. Salt has two primary functions. The number one function is to flavour food. Number two is to preserve. It prevents the process of corruption. Recently it has been used to melt ice on the road to stop cars from crashing. We are to stop men and women crashing into a lost eternity if we are relevant as salt.

The salt covenant we have with The Lord is the Gospel of Jesus Christ. The gospel of Christ is both the salt and light of the world. It both flavours and enlightens the world. The gospel has power to preserve the world from decaying in sin. It is the salt of the earth.

The gospel has power to bring the world out of darkness. It is the light of the world. If the church does not preach the gospel of Christ it will also drown in a world of sin. It goes into captivity under sin's grip.

Matthew 24:14 – And this gospel of the kingdom shall be preached in all the world for a witness unto all nations and then the end will come"

Many churches are preaching their own gospel of prosperity, of spiritual fathers and mothers of healing and deliverance of becoming important in life, of miracles, of getting husbands and material possessions, of empowerment and increase, of following men of God – but the true church will preach the gospel of the King (Jesus) and His domain.

The gospel of the Kingdom is the church's covenant with Christ without which Christ cannot commit Himself to the church. We are called to preach Christ and His Kingdom to all nations amidst religious hypocrisy and betrayal, natural disasters, false prophets, antichrists, spiritual social upheavals, political conflicts and civil wars. The Lord's point was that none of these should stop the preaching of the gospel.

The church should keep focus and the gospel of the kingdom should be the theme. The evils and tribulations mentioned in Matthew 24 are the devil's strategy to intimidate and deceive the church.

Matthew 24:3,4 "And as He sat upon the Mount of Olives, the disciples came to Him privately, saying, Tell us when shall these things be? And what shall be the sign of your coming and the end of the world? And Jesus answered and said to them, Take heed that no man deceive you"

The Lord warned His disciples that they should not let any person deceive them. The preaching of the gospel to all men in the four corners of the world is a big sign that marks the end. Today we have the gospel preached on TV channels to all parts of the world including Islamic nations, the internet, Youtube, Whatapp, Facebook and many social media are being used to channel the gospel so that man has no excuse. The preaching of the gospel of the kingdom marks the end of the world. The gospel will take its course to the end then the end will come. The gospel of the kingdom marks the covenant between Christ and the church.

Matthew 28:19 – "Go ye therefore, and teach all nations, baptising them in the name of The Father and of the Son and of The Holy Spirit.
v20 Teaching them to observe all things that I have commanded you and lo I am with you always, even to the end of the world"

He who does not commit himself to the preaching of the gospel is not one with Christ.

True – The harvest is plenty, but where are the labourers? Many years ago, men farmed lands and harvested crop in baskets but today's technology brings in combine harvesters to gather ripe corn or wheat in much larger quantities. The way we have been preaching is the same with that of a farmer gathering in small baskets but what is in God's heart is to bring in combine harvesters that will gather in an end time harvest of souls. This cannot be the work of men alone but a work of God working through man. His power is behind the harvest. Once we fail to take the crop we lose it to destruction. This sleeping church has to arise and work with The Lord of the harvest. We need to mobilise prayer, work as evangelists, preach the gospel of the kingdom and allow The Holy Spirit to guide us.

The disciples walked with Jesus and their style of preaching was relevant and suitable for the Jewish traditions, but one day they went off shopping. When they came back they found Jesus having a chat with an unusual woman. Very interesting what can come out of Samaria? After Jesus had empowered the no name woman of Samaria she left her water pot – forgot about her physical needs and went back into the city to bring the whole town to Jesus. We are living in that time where God is working through men and women who are willing to lay down their water pots and bring towns and nations to the saviour of all mankind. When I think of this woman of Samaria I feel I will have a conversation with her in heaven. My conversation will go like this – You are blessed, my sister. What a privilege to meet with the Water of Life and oh how He quenched your thirst. One question I would ask is, what is your name? This woman with no name is identified by the geographical location of where she came from. It therefore follows that in each city or village there is one who, if they seek God, can have the capacity to bring the whole town to Jesus. Those who will desire to preach the gospel must first of all receive some water and this water would flow out of them – these are rivers of living water.

The problem we are having is we are rushing off to preach while we are still carrying our water pots. People are distracted by our physical water that they fail to see the supernatural in us. We cannot preach a gospel that suits our lifestyles. We have to let go our previous lifestyles and allow His life in us to manifest.

When people listen to the gospel we preach they need to see authenticity. We have become clowns mimicking one another. The woman put her water pot down so she could acquire greater spiritual grace.

The disciples were learning practical skills on evangelism. Many times we look at people and our judgement of them disqualifies them. God is looking for anyone He can use. What He looks at is not the past but availability. The woman who had had many men was not on the shortlist of clergy and church labourers but God saw an instrument of revival.

THE REASON FOR EVANGELISM

We evangelise simply because it is Christ's passion.

From the age of six I had an unforgettable experience with God. This encounter is very vivid and dear to me. I may not be able to articulate it in this writing – maybe in my next book. I knew from that very young age that God had His hand on me and every day I lived with a knowledge of His presence upon my life. In school, we used to sing this little song:

Jesus wants me for a sunbeam
To shine for Him each day
In every way to try to please Him
At home, at school, at play
A sunbeam A sunbeam
Jesus wants me for a sunbeam
A sunbeam A sunbeam
I will be a sunbeam for Him

To any child this may have been a beautiful little song but for me it was a commitment and a pledge to reflect God's light in a dark world. I grew up with an intense awareness of God's presence in my life and felt a sense of duty to serve Him one day. How I had no clue. As I was growing I never saw female preachers but deep within me was this feeling that one day my life would be dedicated for the Master's use.

I have a lot to say about my childhood but one thing I am always grateful for is that I was raised by a God-fearing mother who took us to church every Sunday in sunshine and rain, winter frost and thunder storms – we had no excuse. Our day started and ended with prayer. My mother was a good role model who preached through her way of life. Every child in the family was dedicated and at the age of fourteen we had to confess Christ and get baptised. There were seven of us and no-one stayed at home on Sunday. We all had to go to church carrying our bibles. If it was raining she would tell us to thank God for sending rain. We would walk in the rain and get to church wet and get on with church business until our clothes dried on us. If anyone was ill she would tell us God is the great physician – we go to church so we can get the healing. She was a real radical believer whose faith was not wavered by the pressures of that day. If my mother had lived in this generation she would have had all children removed from her for what this society would term 'child abuse' but I am grateful for this kind of upbringing because the bible teaches that we are to train children in the way they should go so when they are older they would not depart from that way.

Today we see an antichrist generation where the children are a law unto themselves and do not listen to parental guidance. Any instruction is viewed as abuse.

Isaiah 3:4 "I will give children to be their princes, And babes rule over them.
v5 The people will be oppressed, Everyone by another and everyone by his neighbour. The child will be insolent toward the elder. And the base toward the honourable".
v12 As for my people, children are their oppressors And women rule over them"

The laws that men have made are culturally unacceptable. Today every legislation gives children to rule over parents and we end up with anarchy on our streets. There are few parents today who say to their children, "This is the way – walk in it". Parents collect child benefit and the children become insolent towards their parents. At any tiny form of discipline, they are quick to call the social services so parents live in fear of their children. What a dark time we live in.

As I grew older I religiously went to church even in my backslidden state for I knew no better.

If you lose a coin in the house there is a chance, after thorough cleaning, you may find it. My story is one of that coin that was lost but inside The Father's house. I lived a wayward life but I lingered in the presence of God. I always felt guilty for my worldly living but I never stopped going to church. For a long time I listened to sermons but my heart was dead – nothing moved me. I sort of went to church as a social engagement but yet my heart was far away from God. I sang in the choir, I read the bible but I also sat down to criticise people who gave boring sermons and those whose dressing was not up to standard. I gossiped about everything and everyone. The things that interested me most had nothing to do with Jesus. I followed the crowd and not the cloud. Then one day I had an encounter with The Living God that transformed my life. I am glad I was found lost inside the church but found by a loving God who never gives up on people.

The first thing I wanted to do after my conversion was to read the bible. I made it a mandate to study the bible from Genesis to Revelation. I found out that each day I read the bible I realised how little I knew about Jesus,

I began to ask myself questions like:
- Why did God create me?
- Where is my life going?
- What can I do for God?
- How can I relate to a Holy God?

Each day I would start my prayers with repentance. I realised what a sinner I had been. I would cry my eyes out asking Jesus to wash me in His blood and cleanse me – a hopeless sinner. I would sing this song:

Where would I be if not for You
Where would I go – You only know
A hopeless case
An empty space
If not for Grace

Amazing Grace how sweet the sound
I once was lost but now I'm found
A hopeless case
An empty space
If not for Grace

Looking back, I realised I had played the church game without any relationship with my Saviour and if I had died people would probably have talked about my activities like teaching Sunday school, singing in the choir and paying my tithes but did they know inside I was a wretched sinner on her way to the pits of hell. They would have probably announced that I was a good Christian who never missed a church service, bible study and choir and maybe announced that I had gone to heaven. Reader - do not be deceived. God is not mocked. It's not what people say but our relationship with Jesus is what will take us to heaven.

I was looking for somewhere. My life was written in the bible – then I found it. Luke 4:18-19 "The Spirit of the Lord is upon me, because He has anointed me to preach good news to the poor. He has sent me to proclaim release to the captives and recovering sight to the blind, to set at liberty those who are oppressed, to proclaim the acceptable year of the Lord". And John 20:21 "As the Father has sent me, even I send you".

This became my mission statement. Every day I found someone to share this good news with. All I did was tell them my story of how lost I was in the house of God and yet God found me. I not only preached to the lost world outside church but all those bound by the demon of churchianity.

I was very conscious that God had called me to share His love with others. A sense of direction was fixed in my heart. Before me lay the road of life – much of it hidden but my destination was clear – A call to serve Him till I walk the portals of heaven. Between me and that final goal were souls of men to be harvested. Oh Lord make me your combine harvester like the Samaritan woman!!

I had one thing to do and this was to look at the world and bid it farewell and look heavenward and prayed this simple prayer:

"Lord You created the world from nothing
Here is Maureen nothing
Here is my life – use it"

Oh! I remember that night. It was like drawing a line in the sand and declaring – "devil you will have none of me!" I went to all my worldly friends and preached Christ to them. One man walked into my office and saw the change in me and said, "You don't need to say much I can see it myself!" He knelt down and gave his heart to The Lord and a few days later was taken to glory. I pray I will meet with him one day.

My office at work became a house of prayer. My home was called the upper room – many people gave their lives to Christ. I would talk about

Jesus on the bus and anywhere I went. I look forward to heaven. Each day is a day closer to home.

A LOVE FOR THE WORD

Every day I read the Bible I came across stuff I would love to try out. My pastor saw the change that was on me and now and again would call me to the front to say something. Sometimes it would be a scripture that had blessed me or a testimony that would leave people crying. My pastor was a wonderful bible teacher and every Friday I made it a point to attend the bible study sessions, so sometimes I would just stand up and summarise the wonderful teaching that blessed me.

Soon I was sent to join the team that went out to local farms to evangelise. I would stand there and preach with such zeal and passion that people came crying, as they gave their hearts to Jesus. Many people in the church would ask me how I managed to make such an impact on people but I always knew it was not me. I was just an available vessel that God was using.

As I continued to study my bible I found tools for effective prayer. I had observed my mother praying and fasting for days so I had to walk this road. I began with the three days and three nights dry fasting without taking any fluids. Sometime later I went on to do the forty days on water. Many times people asked me the benefits of those fasts – to be honest I do not know but what I can say is that I have enjoyed good health over the years – never experienced what people call blood pressure, diabetic attacks and all other infirmities. I also found out that fasting was a way of putting the flesh down so the spirit can be nourished. During these days of prayer and fasting I isolated myself and fed on God's word. This gave me a lot of courage and boldness to stand before people.

The people I witnessed to included high ranking government officials and mere peasants. I found that many people wanted me to come and preach in their gatherings. I always asked my pastor before I went and a lot of times he would release me.

My love for the word of God grew and I found myself enrolling at a bible school. This was an American run Rhema bible college which was meant for pastors and other people in leadership roles in their churches. I told them I was neither a pastor nor a leader but one who wanted to study the word of God with help from more qualified people so I would not get into error.

I went to bible school every day after work from 5pm till 9pm which made up 20 hours a week of bible study. I learnt a lot of invaluable stuff from this bible college and just before our graduation there was a guest speaker from America who came to preach. In her preaching, she invited people who desired to be millionaires to come to the front for prayers. I went forward but my prayer went like this:

"Lord this is Maureen
I desire to have a million
Souls in heaven"

I still pray this prayer. For me money will perish but every precious soul won for The Lord will live for eternity. I would rather God give me eternal benefit. Many churches offered me a pastoral position but I had a feeling not to take any appointment.

I went to solitary places to pray and fast and one day was invited to a pastor's conference to preach. I was not a pastor and felt it was out of order to preach to servants of God. The pastor insisted I go so I went. On arrival, the place was packed to capacity – there was no space – then the leader asked me to preach. I asked The Holy Spirit to help me as I shared from John 21:15 where Jesus said to Simon Peter "Simon, son of Jonah, do you love Me more than these?" He said to Him "Lord you know that I love You". He said to him "Feed my lambs". V 16 He said to him again a second time "Simon, son of Jonah do you love Me?" He said to Him "Yes Lord you know that I love You." He said to him "Tend my sheep". V 17 He said to him the third time "Simon, son of Jonah do you love Me?" Peter was grieved because He said to him the third time "Do you love Me?" And he said "Lord, you know all things: You know that I love you". Jesus said to him feed My sheep.

Now Peter had been a fisherman all his life until he met with Jesus just like all of us whom God called we were enjoying our professional jobs when God called us. As a fisherman Peter's job was to catch fish. The moment he encountered Jesus his mission changed. He was to catch men.

In verse 11 Simon dragged the net to the land, full of large fish, one hundred and fifty-three to be precise, and although they were so many the net was not broken.

I always get fascinated when I read the bible. I pick on some revelation. In this particular instance, it was important to put down the number caught in the net, instead of leaving it at a lot of fish. Why was it necessary to record the exact number of the fish caught on this day? I came to realise that during that time there were one hundred and fifty three sovereign nations on the earth and Peter or the disciples' assignment was to take the gospel to every nation. Everything The Lord does is meant to eventually win souls for Him. All the work we do on this earth as ministers of the gospel must end up in adding souls into glory.

One of the primary ministries of The Holy Spirit is to bring conviction to people's hearts. We are called to do our bit which is feeding then The Holy Spirit will do the convincing. He makes the word we preach alive so men are convicted.

Jesus asked Peter: "Do you love me?" And that is the one question He is asking us today. If I were Jesus maybe on that day I would have asked Peter – Do you realise how I felt when you denied Me three times – three times in front of my enemies? Maybe I would have gone further to ask 'Peter have you not heard of deliverance ministry where they deliver liars from their lives?' Or – 'How could I trust you with ministry when I'm gone when you behave like this in my presence?' Oh what a wonderful God.

Jesus was saying to Peter I know your faults but do you have a passion in your heart to carry on with this journey? Jesus knows that in our walk as ministers we will stumble but after we stumble do we love Him enough to rise again and serve Him without looking into the rear-view mirror.

This is a question that The Lord has for all of us running on this heaven-bound track. Our passion must not die due to pressures and challenges of this world. Our passion for The Lord should never die. Many things might work to rob or erode our love for Jesus. Such things as stress, failure, pleasure, sin, material possession or lack of, sickness, divorce, separation and many others but we go back to God and cry out for restoration. We pursue intimacy with The Lord after every fall. We draw closer to Him not walk away. We admit our short-comings and ask for His help. He promised never to leave nor forsake us. Tommy Tenney, a revivalist and author of the 'God Chasers' writes 'God is everywhere, but He doesn't turn His face and His favour everywhere. That is why He tells us to seek His face. Yes, He is present with you every time you meet with other believers in a worship service but how long has it been since your hunger caused you to crawl up on His lap, and like a child, to reach up and take the face of God to turn it toward you. Intimacy with Him – that is what God desires.

Tenny, Tommy The God Chasers (Shippensburg, PA: Destiny Image Publishers ,1998) p 38.

Peter was being called to that kind of dedication 'Do you love me?' When we read Psalm 24:6 'This is Jacob, the generation of those who seek Him'. Who seek your face" Jacob is a flawed character who singled himself out by the nature of his relationship with God. He, despite weakness, wrestled with God for a blessing. We are called to that place where our victory only comes through a personal relationship with the one who called us. A generation of leaders who seek God as Jacob did. With a sense of desperation we seek His presence without which our labour is fruitless.

Jesus died so that we no longer live for ourselves. The woman at the Samaritan well left her water pot (her physical needs) and went on to work for the greater need of others which was salvation.

Jesus was asking Peter if he loved Him and was passionate about Him. This would reflect on his commitment to the community. Jesus died for us all "that those who lived should no longer live for themselves but for Him who died for them and was raised again" 2 Corinthians 5:15. This is not just a need to be humbled by our weaknesses. It is more an issue of always realising our need of Jesus. The only reason why we serve Him is because He called us. Peter was being called and today we are called by Him to serve. I warn anyone who gives into this work with no clarity of call. Peter was being directed to service and this was to feed the lambs. Our ultimate goal is to please the one who called us and not people around us. We owe our lives to Him because He died for us. Together with Peter I find myself saying 'Lord you know all things. You know I love You.'

My love for Him should increase my passion for His service. Passion becomes the fuel for conviction about the gospel of Jesus Christ as 'the power of God for the salvation of all those who believe' (Romans 1:16). My message went on to describe the need for a personal love for Christ rather than just theological training. Jesus did not say: Peter do you love Me – go to theological college. Our calling is defined by Jesus and our passion for His work increases when we love Him. People are watching us and the only way we can make an impact in their lives is when we are in love with Jesus.

Paul, a newcomer and apostle of Jesus had great conviction about his gospel and consuming love for Christ when he wrote 'I consider everything as loss, compared to the surpassing greatness of knowing Christ Jesus my Lord, for whose sake I have lost all things. (Philippians 3:8). A flame of constant love consumed Paul. This should be our foundational value. Serving God should not be a casual routine but a passionate service out of love for Jesus.

The Samaritan woman had gone to the well to meet her physical need. All her life had been spent on finding physical affection. If the need was not satisfied by husband number one then maybe number two had all the answers. Little did she know that no man can satisfy a spiritual need. Her search for love got her to husband number five and yet the story remained the same. Remember Christ crying on Calvary 'I thirst' – it was not mere water He was talking about. His whole mission to earth was to find a bride – one He would present to His Father as spotless, without spot or wrinkle. If there was any other way to do it He would have followed that route but He had to die and death on a cross of shame. He had an unquenchable thirst – one that could only be satisfied by the true bride. The Samaritan woman's search was over when she met with the living water. She left her water pot and carried a passion compared to none. A love for the one who had taken away her thirst. This was no ordinary water. The well burst forth from within her and she was now on a mission to let these waters flow out of her and touch the whole city. She cried out in the streets of Samaria "Come see a man". All Samaria had known this woman with different men yet what drove her now was a new passion. The whole city came to see face to face with the living water. That is to be our way of service if we are to serve God.

People look at us as we deliver dead messages – most of them copied from other preachers. What we fail to realise is that people are spiritual beings we may have a beautiful sermon that only touches the head and not the heart. Anything born from love will touch hearts of men. Every preacher should be motivated by love otherwise our labour is in vain. Remember Jesus' priestly prayer in John 17 V 26 – He petitioned The Father 'that the love you have for me may be in them and that I myself may be in them'. Is there any higher privilege than to share with God The Father the same passion He has for His Son as we engage with His call to follow Him?

REACHING THE LOST

When Jesus instructed Peter, "feed my lambs" many have seen this as preaching the gospel to the young in spirit, those who are coming to the Lord for the first time, those who are just fresh from the world. Jesus displayed an attitude of compassion when He dealt with unbelievers. Matthew 9:36 "He had compassion on them because they were harassed and helpless" When we are looking after babies – the diet we give them is soft and mostly liquid, because their system cannot cope with hard stuff. God has placed on us a mandate to consider the level of each person as they come to know Christ. At the first level we give them milk which is the word of God.

Isaiah 28:9 "Whom will He teach knowledge? And whom will He make to understand the message
v10 – "For precept must be upon precept, line upon line. Here a little, there a little." We depend on God to teach us how to preach to His people.
v27 – For black cumin is not threshed with a threshing sledge. Nor is a cartwheel rolled over cumin, but the black cumin is beaten out with a stick. And the cumin with a rod.
v29 – This also comes from The Lord of Hosts who is wonderful in counsel and excellent in guidance.

Just as the farmer brings in a crop for his efforts, according to the wisdom God has instilled in him. God's activities with people, shepherds have a purpose – to bring in spiritual crop.

GOD WANTS US BLESSED

James gives us a definition of true religion. True religion according to Apostle James will issue pure speech, pure love and pure character. James does not give an exhaustive list of the positive duties of genuine religion but he presents these as typical characteristics. James 1:27 – "Pure and undefiled religion before God The Father is this: to visit orphans and widows in their trouble and to keep oneself unspotted from the world". God challenges us to a heart of serving the helpless. Those things closest to the Father's heart, the things He views as precious revolve around caring for the needy and personal holiness. God's majesty and power are best understood in light of His tender compassion toward orphans and widows. When His children care for the distressed their actions are pure and faultless in God's view because they reflect His heart. We should evangelise, fast, study the word and pray but our looking out for and defending the helpless brings pleasure to God without qualification.

God wants us blessed, prospered and happy. He has no problems with me living where I want, eating what I want to eat. Why does He want me blessed? - So that I will have more than enough to give unto every good work and charitable donations.

The primary purpose of divine provision is to enable us to fulfil the purpose for which we were created. Poverty is not a sin but it is definitely not the will of God for His children. When Abraham was called, he was given a promise of a <u>blessing</u> – now the blessing is not money but it attracts wealth.
Genesis 12:1-3 – Now The Lord had said to Abram 'Get out of your country, from your family and from your father's house, to the land I will show you. I will make you a great nation. I will <u>bless</u> you and make your name great, and you shall be a <u>blessing</u>. I will bless those who bless you and I will curse him who curses you. And in you all the families of the earth shall be blessed through you'.

The first blessing for Abram was not money but a name – God had in mind a messianic nation that would bring salvation to all earth's families. God did in many ways bless Abram including material blessing. Galatians 3 V 13 – God promises to give all believers the blessing of Abraham for Jesus became a curse for us so we may receive the blessing of Abraham. This begins with being born again. God wants us to prosper spiritually first, emotionally, physically and materially.

God's will is that we have enough resources to fulfil dreams in our heart. Either dreams formulated by independent thought or which have been mediated to us by The Holy Spirit as the will of God. If God puts in my heart a desire to go and preach and I fail because I don't have (petrol) transport money this is not God's will but a manifestation of the grip of poverty.

When God called me to live by faith for four years I knew it was not His will for me to sign up on benefits. It was the same time He called me to look for an office in the centre of town. I had no bank balance in my account to show anyone for the approval of an office. I knew the state would look after me if I went to apply for benefits but I felt I was called to look after the affairs of the state not the other way round. I don't think it is God's will for Christians to be on benefits, then how different are we from the world? It is not a sin to be on benefits but the world will not see the need for God if the state can do the same.

God never wants His people running to the world for solutions but rather the world running to God – or to the church for permanent solutions. Genesis 49:29-33 – Abraham offered to buy land even burial ground he did not accept freebees!!

God wants His Mountain exalted above other mountains. So that the world – all nations will run to the house of the Lord. In the church in the book of Acts no-one had any need – those who had gave to the ones who did not have. Church members should help each other, then the community outside will be drawn to the house of God – a house of bread. They can then have their spiritual hunger met as well. Paul was always encouraging saints to meet the needs of those in Jerusalem. We need to start practicing what we teach to love one another. Poverty is not a blessing as are sickness and sin but these can be eradicated by the blood of Jesus.

During my times of living by faith God raised men and women of God to minister into my life. Some sowed money into my account every month and others gave me cars. This is what God wants to see among fellow believers.

The teaching of The Cross is meant to set God's standard in us as Christians. When we teach a wholesome word it affects the spiritual person and produces the physical needs we have.

One day I was crying to God for a car. The Lord nudged me to trust Him for a brand new car. It is the same faith that we have for an old car. Faith produces a material blessing. At the time I was not working but working full time in a non paying ministry. I had no payslip to prove any income – my bank account was minus three thousand. I was overdrawn. No one could give me a loan – not even for a phone. I had tried to go to the Ford garage to get a car worth £7 thousand but they had rejected it outright.

I would like to point out here that it's not our salary that produces results but our faith in God does. Some people have large salaries yet remain tenants while others earn average salaries and are home owners. The blessing of God makes one rich and faith in God works in our favour.

During this time in my life I had a lot to learn from God. I learnt that it is not good credit rating that produces results – it is not that rating that gives one a mortgage. If one has a good credit rating then there is no testimony there. I'm not however advocating poor credit ratings but that all things belong to God and God wants us blessed so we can testify of His goodness and fulfil our callings. Blessings are not for the carnal proud display and for despising those that don't have but a testimony of the goodness of our God so others may believe in Him.

I felt The Lord say "A thousand cattle on a hill belong to me – even the hills are mine". Then I heard – "Go to Toyota and get a brand-new car". I started to laugh like Sarah. I thought I had gone to the Ford garage to get a second-hand car and they had disqualified me, now Toyota cars are more expensive they would just laugh at me. I knew it was The Lord so I went. When I got there I met a very pleasant man called Nigel. This man asked me about my profession which I mentioned as a pastor of a young church. This man asked for my bank statement, which was overdrawn, and my driver's licence which I gave to him and waited. He went upstairs to an office and downstairs I started to speak in tongues. I waited for the usual – "sorry madam – your application is not successful this time" The waiting seemed forever. My faith was being tested. I kept looking at the beautiful cars. In my heart, I chose one that I could use to carry people to church and the colour should be red. It was a seven seater of that same year 2014 and in my heart the matter was settled. Nigel came down smiling. He told me my finance had been approved. I was shocked and wondered who on earth would approve of an amount of £21,000 for someone like me? I asked them who had given me the money and he said it was the Toyota finance. This man asked me what car I wanted so I described the seven seater Avensis – red in colour. He took me outside to show me and all I could do was cry. This man looked at me as I wept in my heart thanking God for His faithfulness. He gave me the keys and set up my phone on Bluetooth and personalised everything in my name. He gave me a date to pay the finances monthly into the Toyota account. As I drove off home I testified of God's goodness.

From the day I got the car finances started coming in. I have never failed to pay that amount every month.

I realised money is not an end in itself but a means to an end. We use money to gain souls into the kingdom. We need money for evangelism and to do missionary work. We need to look after widows and orphans. We need to buy bibles and give to those who have not read the word. Yes, we need money to 'occupy till He comes'. The little we give to mission projects will win souls for eternity.

We use money to build God's kingdom, Haggai 1:1-15 – "In the second year of King Darius, in the sixth month, on the first day of the month, the word of The Lord came by Haggai the prophet to Zerubbabel, the son of Shealtiel, governor of Judah and to Joshua son of Jozadak, the high priest saying: (2) Thus speaks the Lord of hosts, saying, "This people says the time has not come, the time that the Lord's house should be built." (3) "Is it time for you yourselves to dwell in your panelled houses, and this temple to lie in ruins?" Now therefore, thus, says the Lord of hosts: "Consider your ways! You have sown much, and bring in little. You eat, but do not have enough; you drink, but you are not filled with drink; you clothe yourselves but no-one is warm. And he, who earns wages, earns wages to put in a bag with holes." (7) Thus says the Lord of hosts, "Consider your ways! (8) Go up to the mountains and bring wood and build the temple that I may take pleasure in it and be glorified" says the Lord. (9) "You looked for much, but indeed it came to little, and when you brought it home, I blew it away. Why?" says the Lord of hosts. "Because of My house that is in ruins, while every one of you runs to his own house. (10) Therefore the heavens above you withhold the dew, and the earth withholds its fruit."

God is looking at the church and calling it to put Him first in all things.

God is acting to help His people to establish proper priorities. Sixteen years earlier people had started to rebuild the temple and then they had lost the zeal and passion. Is that not how we all start out, attending all church services, Monday intercession, Tuesday choir practice, Wednesday mid-week service, Thursday outreach and coffee mornings, Friday bible study, Saturday decorating the church and Sunday early service and late service. Then we start off by missing the choir and then the intercession until we become Sunday Christians or even worse – fair-weather Christians – we only go to church when it's not raining, when we are feeling well, when we wake up on the right side of the bed. We do this until we die down to, "I will pray at home". We have lost our drive, our zeal and passion. There is no more vision and motivation. Then we start to fulfil our own agendas.

When we look at the above scriptures we must respond with true repentance and obedience. God has not called us as a crowd but as individuals who are willing to be part of His big plan. We need to work in unity with others until we build an army for the Lord. Each man should start with a resolution to commence building God's house.

The house of God must come first. The word of The Lord must come first. Only then can we claim the blessings of God. I have learnt over the years to read God's word every day - at least ten chapters a day – and read the whole bible at least once a year and fast at least once a week and at least one month a year.

God wants us blessed but the single non-negotiable condition for His blessing is that His kingdom, His programme and His work must come first in our lives and thoughts. Reading His word every day guides us into all truths. Fasting helps us focus on the spiritual person and helps the spiritual man to be in tune with the Holy Spirit. This helps us to break free from the world system.

Chapter 10

Take stock of your life

For many years I played the <u>blame game</u>. If anything was lost I found someone or situation to blame. There was never a time I stopped to look at myself and ask why I found myself in ugly situations. Looking back at my life I have seen that I lost a lot of opportunities to do with education and employment. I have lost money, friends and vital relationships.

There is a promise of God's restoration for those who know what they have lost. I like to make a list and show the Lord of what I have lost. Joel 2:23-25: "I will restore to you the years that the swarming locust has eaten. The crawling locust, the chewing locust." Take stock of what was stolen how can you have no clue you have lost anything. Make a list of what was stolen and what you have dropped by the wayside. My daughter would always remind me how anointed I was, how powerful the message I preached, how many people I touched. It used to make me angry but after considering those words I was able to come up with a list of all the things that were stolen in my life and I found that I had lost:

1) Joy
2) Peace
3) Love
4) Fellowship with The Holy Spirit
5) Prayer time
6) Fasting
7) Evangelism
8) Zeal
9) Passion
10) Relationship with God
11) Reading my bible
12) Personal evangelism
13) Visiting the sick
14) Giving to the poor
15) Studying
16) Fellowship with others
17) Energy
18) Interest.

The next thing to look at was what caused this to happen? Among other things is friendship with the world. We are living under such pressure to be acceptable to the world. Trying to appeal to the dictates of this world and associating with worldly friends. The bible says do not be deceived – bad company corrupts good manners.

It's important to take time to evaluate our walk and our lives in general. The devil is a thief who comes to steal, kill and destroy – John 10:10

It's important to take stock of all things that cause us to lose our anointing because we can lose it. Saul was anointed and yet God rejected him. Look at your prayer life – are you spending more time in the presence of The Lord or watching TV.

Fight for your anointing and gifting, cry out to God for restoration. What has happened to the miracles? Why are we speaking in the past – oh I used to fast forty days and forty nights – what is happening now?

What has happened to all the people God brought into your life to serve with you? It's not everyone that God removed – some were removed because of competition and insecurity. Fight for good relationships, friends, in-laws, children and bosses. Protect those relationships. Remember the devil hides behind our relatives so we start fighting with each other. When was the last time you prayed for your family members, cousins, friends and neighbours? Instead of pointing out their faults pray for them.

As a church, we need to come together to pray for stolen members, relatives and marriages that have been lost to the enemy. The Holy Spirit is the one who can reveal to us what was stolen. He gives us the anointing to pray to recover. That is watching and praying.

SEEK YE THE KINGDOM

We live in perilous times where values have been grossly reversed. All wickedness is called good today and all good is seen as evil. Many years ago if you said you were a Christian this would earn you respect but today that word calls for resentment, ridicule and even death in some parts of the world. It is in a time like this that we are being called to seek the Kingdom of God. This cannot be seen by human eyes but it is of the heart.

We live in a material world where competition is rife even in the church people want to show off their material acquisitions.

Matthew 6:25 says "Therefore I say to you, do not worry about your life, what you will eat or what you will drink; not about your body, what you will put on. Is life not more than food and the body more than clothing? (33) But seek first the kingdom of God and His righteousness and all these things shall be added to you." Worry means a distraction, a preoccupation with things that cause anxiety, stress and pressure. Jesus speaks against worry and anxiety because of the watchful care of a heavenly Father who is ever mindful of our daily needs. Jesus teaches us how to live in uncertain financial times, without fear or stress. We are not to be distracted. We are the only creation of God that worries – birds don't worry.

Instead of worrying we are encouraged to seek the Kingdom of God and His righteousness. The word Kingdom can be split into two: it's to do with a King, in this case "Christ", and "dom", His domain. The Kingdom is of righteousness, peace and joy in The Holy Spirit. It is about a total willingness to surrender to Jesus Christ and to make Him Lord over every aspect of our lives – making Him overall Supreme Master of our lives. It is about a determination to make heaven and live a life with heaven in view and a willingness to suffer and lose all just to attain heaven. We are called to live as if we were dying tomorrow - living at peace with all men and in love with the Living God.

The Kingdom view is that of walking the narrow path that leads to eternal life and this is the direct opposite of the new age Christianity which focuses on being rich, powerful, influential, wealthy and all the rest. For some people Jesus died to make them millionaires. I don't think so. If that were the case then all rich Arabs and drug dealers would qualify to go to heaven on the grounds of their material wealth. On the contrary we Christians acquire our blessing from Christ's suffering on the cross where our sinful nature is dealt with and we have a new identity to walk His walk until we make heaven. Money alone is not a sign of God's favour or lack of it a sign of God's punishment. There are many rich robbers, fraudsters and human traffickers who have great wealth but this is not a sign of God's blessing. Jesus did not leave buildings and investments because He came to invest in one investment 'The Human Soul'. Today it is very sad to see great men and women of God selling books on:-

How to be rich
How to be powerful
How to be influential.

They have forgotten the narrow path that leads to heaven. There is a lot of greed and covetousness where men market their preachings and seminars for money. Men of God have become self-seeking and self-promoting. Their churches have become market places where they trade their wares, books, CDs, training manuals, and each man markets their product to the flock. Jesus one day went into the temple and overturned tables. Today every programme and church even is tailor made to make money and no-one speaks of heaven anymore or warns people of hellfire.

We are called to seek The Kingdom and walk the narrow way. We cannot make our own rules but take God's rules and in this narrow way we get rid of all baggage. Galatians 5 talks of the baggage we need to get rid of; adultery, fornication, uncleanness, lewdness, idolatry, sorcery, hatred, contentions, jealousies, outbursts of wrath, selfish ambitions, dissensions, heresies, envy, murder, drunkenness, revelries – those who practice these will not inherit the Kingdom of God. More baggage of unforgiveness, open mindedness, tolerance – we need to get rid of these. The narrow path calls us to change in behaviour and this is not easy at all. In the broad way or wide gate people do what they want, believe whatever they want, live however they want without any constraints. Wide is the gate that leads to destruction.

People will say God is very gracious. He will not destroy the whole world but we know in the time of Noah millions were lost in the flood. Only Noah and seven other people who walked the narrow way survived. When the children of Israel sinned against God millions were lost in the wilderness and only two people who had left Egypt entered Canaan. That was Joshua and Caleb and the new generation born in the wilderness that had no clue of Egypt. When The Lord visited Sodom and Gomorrah He rescued only three people out of that wicked place. God is not moved by numbers but He honours those who choose His way.

The destination board is clear, one is for destruction for those who ignore the message of the cross. Jesus does not offer us an ordinary life but a life of self-denial so we may enter eternity. He wants us to take up His throne in our hearts and rule. He wants us to live a life free from sin. We have a choice to let Him reign or choose the wide path which leads to destruction. Dropping the baggage is not easy because we are used to it. It's our comfort zone. When I watch that programme of hoarders I'm surprised by what they say. They are buried in rubbish clutter and when you try to help them declutter they just ask you to put it outside after a while they go back to bring that rubbish in until they are buried in it. They love the clutter – it's a place of safety. They are used to seeing it every day. The lies that make it easy to explain why we are late for work. The green eye when our friends are doing better than us exposing our enemies make us look better than them. God wants all that clutter to go. The road He has called us is too narrow for baggage.

Sometimes it is our friends we need to let go. 1Corinthians 5:9 "I wrote to you in my epistle not to <u>keep company</u> with sexually immoral people" This is not meaning people of the world because we need to reach out to them but (11) anyone named a brother, who is sexually immoral, or covetous, or an idolater, or a reviler, or a drunkard or an extortioner – not even to eat with such people. We need to let some relationships go but continue to pray for such people.

We have a promised kingdom to inherit. We need to learn how to live as citizens of that heavenly kingdom all our earthly baggage will go. 1Corinthians 6: 9 – "Do you not know that the unrighteous will not inherit the kingdom of God? Do not be deceived. Neither fornicators, nor idolaters, nor adulterers, nor homosexuals, nor sodomites, nor thieves, nor covetous, nor drunkards, nor revilers, nor extortioners will inherit the kingdom of God"

All the evil doers mentioned can be washed clean from sin if they accept Christ as their Lord and Saviour. Jesus does not condemn anyone who truly believes in Him. His arms are open to receive one who will call upon His name.

One day in a dream I was taken to a place where I saw people walk towards a destination. They were many people walking in a beautiful wide road with full of choices – they were so many no-one could count them. Towards the end of that road were loud screams of pain and agony and darkness. There was also a narrow road. Very few people walked on this way and they suffered a lot but their destination was a beautiful peaceful place of colours and song.

The narrow way leads to life full of pain, suffering, sacrifice and obedience. The wide road leads to destruction. It is full of riches, choices – many walk it. Jesus says I am the way. The truth and the life – no-one comes to the Father except through Me. Are you going among the many or the few? Be ready to sacrifice – it means changes it is not easy but can be done. It's not too late to open your heart and let the King come in to have His domain in you.

LAST DAYS

Jesus Christ taught that the last days shall be characterised by much iniquity, hatred of God, natural disasters, intensified satanic activity, backsliding, false prophets and demonic miracle workers and mockery of rapture. Yet these last days also shall be characterised with the outpouring of The Holy Spirit upon men and women for explosive gospel work and the gospel of Jesus Christ will be preached on TV, internet, twitter, whatsapp and all media. The pure remnant preachers will be there despite hardship, torture, persecution and challenges. True Christians will persevere to the end. Matthew 24:1,4-14.

2 Peter 3:1-14 – "This second epistle, beloved I now write to you; in both which I stir up your pure minds by way of remembrance (2) That you may be mindful of the words which were spoken before by the holy prophets and the commandments of us the apostles of the Lord and Saviour (3) Knowing this first, that there shall come in the last days scoffers, walking after their own lusts (4) and saying 'Where is the promise of His coming?' For since our fathers fell asleep, all things continue as they were from the beginning of the creation (5) For this they willingly are ignorant of, that by the word of God the heavens were of old, and the earth standing out of the water and is water. Whereby the world that then was being overflowed with water perished (7) But the heavens and the earth, which

are now by the same word are kept in store, reserved unto fire again the day of judgement and perdition of ungodly men. (8) But beloved, be not be ignored of this one thing, that one day is with the Lord as a thousand years, and a thousand years as one day. (9) The Lord is not slack concerning His promise, as some men count slackness; but is long suffering toward us, not willing that any should perish, but that all should come to repentance (10) But the day of the Lord will come like a thief in the night; in which the heavens shall pass away with a great noise, and the elements shall melt with fervent heat, the earth also and the works that are therein shall be burned up. (11) Seeing then that all these things shall be dissolved, what manner of persons ought you to be in all holy conversation and godliness (12) Looking for and hasting unto the coming of the day of God, wherein the heavens being on fire shall be dissolved and the elements shall melt with fervent heat? (13) Nevertheless we according to His promise look for new heavens and a new earth where righteousness dwells. (14) Therefore beloved, seeing that we look for such things, be diligent that you may be found of Him in peace, without spot, and blameless"

Jesus preached that one day He would return to capture His saints in the sky. He shall descend from heaven with His angels and the saints now in heaven with a shout, with the voice of the archangel. The trumpet of God shall sound. The Lord will remain in the air. Every eye shall see him the dead and the living will see Him. Even those that pierced Him shall see Him in His glory. The saints who came with Him from heaven shall return to the earth to be reunited with their bodies – they shall resurrect with glorious bodies – the sea will give up all the dead and the graves will open up to let them go. Those scattered as ashes will come together to a glorious body. The saints living on earth shall be suddenly changed and transformed with a glorious eternal body with no sickness, no pain, no handicap and no old age. They shall rise up to meet their Lord in the air. The Lord shall take them all back to heaven for the marriage supper and give them eternal rewards according to their works. This is a message meant to comfort all believers.

1 Thessalonians 4:13-18
2 Thessalonians 2:3-10

After the saints are taken into heaven there is going to be a great tribulation on this earth.

Revelations 13:1-18
Revelations 16:1-18
Zachariah 14:1-7
Revelations 19:11-21

The saints go to heaven and chaos never seen before creation of humanity takes hold of the whole earth - a period of unequalled suffering, hardship and persecution. God will visit the earth with serious divine judgement for all those who rejected Christ Jesus. In this period the antichrist will show up physically as a representative of Satan. He shall persecute the Christians who have not made it at rapture - because some Christians who are not walking in the ways of God and not ready for the rapture will remain on earth. The antichrist will persecute these saints and the nation of Israel. He shall declare Himself as God and demand to be worshipped. He shall cause men to take the mark 666 on their foreheads and the right hand men will not buy or sell without that mark. Take heed if you are left behind, my brother and sister, I beg you with the mercy of God do not take this mark on you. If you have to die for Christ this is the only option for once the mark is on you, you have lost all hope for eternal hope. The Lord Jesus shall defeat the antichrist.

The Lord Jesus shall return visibly to earth as the King of Kings and Lord of Lords. Those who have kept themselves pure will meet with Him. Those who reject Him will go to a place of total separation and real place of torture and torment called hell. Everlasting burning and torment which God never intended for human beings but for Satan and his demons but men go there by their own choice of rejecting Christ, the only Saviour of the world. All dead sinners shall be resurrected back to life and shall be judged according to their works when they were alive on earth and shall be condemned into the lake of fire. Hell itself will be cast into the lake of fire. The habitants of the lake of fire will be Satan, his demons and father of angels and sinners who rejected Christ. This will be the end of rebellion.

Mark 9:43-48
Revelation 20:10-15

HEAVEN

Song: *In the land of fadeless day*

In the land of fadeless day
Lies the city foursquare;
It shall never pass away,
And there is no night there.

- *Refrain:*
  God shall wipe away all tears,
  There's no death, no pain, nor fears,
  And they count not time by years,
  For there is no night there.

"For behold, I create new heavens and a new earth;
And the former shall not be remembered or come to mind.
[18] But be glad and rejoice forever in what I create;
For behold, I create Jerusalem *as* a rejoicing,
And her people a joy.
[19] I will rejoice in Jerusalem,
And joy in My people;
The voice of weeping shall no longer be heard in her,
Nor the voice of crying.

Isaiah 65:17-19

The Lord is not slack concerning *His* promise, as some count slackness, but is longsuffering toward us not willing that any should perish but that all should come to repentance.

[10] But the day of the Lord will come as a thief in the night, in which the heavens will pass away with a great noise, and the elements will melt with fervent heat; both the earth and the works that are in it will be burned up. [11] Therefore, since all these things will be dissolved, what manner *of*

persons ought you to be in holy conduct and godliness, [12] looking for and hastening the coming of the day of God, because of which the heavens will be dissolved, being on fire, and the elements will melt with fervent heat? [13] Nevertheless we, according to His promise, look for new heavens and a new earth in which righteousness dwells.

[14] Therefore, beloved, looking forward to these things, be diligent to be found by Him in peace, without spot and blameless;

2 Peter 3:9-14

Now I saw a new heaven and a new earth, for the first heaven and the first earth had passed away. Also there was no more sea. [2] Then I, John, saw the holy city, New Jerusalem, coming down out of heaven from God, prepared as a bride adorned for her husband. [3] And I heard a loud voice from heaven saying, "Behold, the tabernacle of God *is* with men, and He will dwell with them, and they shall be His people. God Himself will be with them *and be* their God. [4] And God will wipe away every tear from their eyes; there shall be no more death, nor sorrow, nor crying. There shall be no more pain, for the former things have passed away."

[5] Then He who sat on the throne said, "Behold, I make all things new." And He said to me, "Write, for these words are true and faithful."

[6] And He said to me, "It is done! I am the Alpha and the Omega, the Beginning and the End. I will give of the fountain of the water of life freely to him who thirsts. [7] He who overcomes shall inherit all things, and I will be his God and he shall be My son. [8] But the cowardly, unbelieving, abominable, murderers, sexually immoral, sorcerers, idolaters, and all liars shall have their part in the lake which burns with fire and brimstone, which is the second death."

[9] Then one of the seven angels who had the seven bowls filled with the seven last plagues came to me and talked with me, saying, "Come, I will show you the bride, the Lamb's wife." [10] And he carried me away in the Spirit to a great and high mountain, and showed me the great city, the holy Jerusalem, descending out of heaven from God, [11] having the glory of God. Her light *was* like a most precious stone, like a jasper stone, clear as crystal. [12] Also she had a great and high wall with twelve gates, and

twelve angels at the gates, and names written on them, which are *the names* of the twelve tribes of the children of Israel: [13] three gates on the east, three gates on the north, three gates on the south, and three gates on the west.

[14] Now the wall of the city had twelve foundations, and on them were the names of the twelve apostles of the Lamb. [15] And he who talked with me had a gold reed to measure the city, its gates, and its wall. [16] The city is laid out as a square; its length is as great as its breadth. And he measured the city with the reed: twelve thousand furlongs. Its length, breadth, and height are equal. [17] Then he measured its wall: one hundred *and* forty-four cubits, *according* to the measure of a man, that is, of an angel. [18] The construction of its wall was *of* jasper; and the city *was* pure gold, like clear glass. [19] The foundations of the wall of the city *were* adorned with all kinds of precious stones: the first foundation *was* jasper, the second sapphire, the third chalcedony, the fourth emerald, [20] the fifth sardonyx, the sixth sardius, the seventh chrysolite, the eighth beryl, the ninth topaz, the tenth chrysoprase, the eleventh jacinth, and the twelfth amethyst. [21] The twelve gates *were* twelve pearls: each individual gate was of one pearl. And the street of the city *was* pure gold, like transparent glass.

[22] But I saw no temple in it, for the Lord God Almighty and the Lamb are its temple. [23] The city had no need of the sun or of the moon to shine in it, for the glory of God illuminated it. The Lamb *is* its light. [24] And the nations of those who are saved shall walk in its light, and the kings of the earth bring their glory and honor into it. [25] Its gates shall not be shut at all by day (there shall be no night there). [26] And they shall bring the glory and the honor of the nations into it. [27] But there shall by no means enter it anything that defiles, or causes an abomination or a lie, but only those who are written in the Lamb's Book of Life.

Revelation 21:1-27

Heaven is the home of our God. It is perfect and glorious, delightful, comfortable and peaceful. It is Holy and everlasting. It is the home of angels, living creatures and saints who have departed in Christ. Jesus calls it My Father's house with many mansions. He promised to prepare a place for you and me and come back to take us there. He wants to give us rewards and crowns for all our good work on earth.

"Let not your heart be troubled; you believe in God, believe also in Me. [2] In My Father's house are many mansions; if *it were* not *so,* I would have told you. I go to prepare a place for you. [3] And if I go and prepare a place for you, I will come again and receive you to Myself; that where I am, *there* you may be also. [4] And where I go you know, and the way you know."

[5] Thomas said to Him, "Lord, we do not know where You are going, and how can we know the way?"

[6] Jesus said to him, "I am the way, the truth, and the life. No one comes to the Father except through Me.

John 14:1-6

These all died in faith, not having received the promises, but having seen them afar off were assured of them, embraced *them* and confessed that they were strangers and pilgrims on the earth. [14] For those who say such things declare plainly that they seek a homeland. [15] And truly if they had called to mind that *country* from which they had come out, they would have had opportunity to return. [16] But now they desire a better, that is, a heavenly *country.* Therefore God is not ashamed to be called their God, for He has prepared a city for them.

Hebrews 11:13-16

My friend make up your mind today to accept Jesus as your Lord and saviour and ask The Holy Spirit to help you walk with Him till we meet in that glorious home where there is no sorrow, pain or death. Marantha!

About the author

Maureen Mataranyika was born in a small town of Rusape Makoni District in Zimbabwe to William and Sophia Mataranyika.

"My childhood was very much influenced by her mother who was promoted to glory in July 2012. She was a strong Christian who practised her faith before us. When we got sick she prayed for us; although my father worked in the hospital she would not allow us to take medication directing every need to Jesus who became The Healer we all saw. She taught us to pray if we needed anything and we went to church almost daily. For intercession on Monday, Tuesday was evangelism, Wednesday house group, Thursday choir, Friday bible study and Saturday youth meeting, Sunday all day at church!

At the tender age of six I was very aware of God and knew one day l would serve Him. My mother confirmed this and started calling me *Chimoto* (Trans: A flame of fire). I loved God with all my heart and for a long time felt my only calling was to give and pray. I trained as a teacher and taught in Girls High School, Harare and Lord Malvern High School Harare, Zimbabwe. l also worked for the Curriculum Development Unit in Zimbabwe at which point The Lord called me into full time ministry. I trained with Rhema Bible School and served as a pastor before l came to the UK. I was involved with spiritual mapping of Zimbabwe and travelled to every town city and village praying for revival and repenting for the sin of the nation . In 2002 l came to the UK and taught in several schools before l was called into praying for the nation in 2007; this was the birth of Ignite Global Prayer Ministries. With a few ladies meeting in my house we prayed every morning for revival. There was such a burden in me to cry out for this great nation that had faithfully given the gospel to us in Africa. I remember that when David Livingstone died he asked that his heart be buried in Livingstone, Zambia and his body taken to Scotland. At that time Zimbabwe and Zambia were one country so spiritually his heart is in my country; I feel this is pay- back time, God had brought me here with a specific assignment to pray for this nation.

Ecclesiastes 11:1 "Cast your bread upon many waters after many days it will come back to you"

This to me was the calling that we come to re-evangelize those that gave us the Gospel. From 2007 God gave me a strategy to pray in every town releasing the atmosphere for coming revivals. Starting with Bristol, then Wales I have been to more than 70 towns of the UK praying for revival.

15 Agate Court Sonora Fields Sittingbourne Kent ME10 5LF

Answers to prayers – meeting with two of God's servants

This is me a short while ago with Andrew White the vicar of Baghdad I had gone to Liverpool to preach and pray for revival in the land and had this God moment. For many years I have been praying for the vicar of Baghdad with a few intercessors and one day I had prayed and asked God oh l hope one day in heaven l would meet up with this vicar and listen to what he has to say about all his persecutions for the Gospel of Christ. God has a sense of humour He did not have to wait but created this time for me to meet him heard him teach and sat down for a chat wow what a mighty God we serve

That's me and Jackie Pulling at Ashburnham last year 2016 l had made a similar prayer my son Robert had bought me a book by Jackie Pullinger. I had read it and felt really challenged l felt l needed to do more for God and this woman really inspired me so l prayed the same simple prayer Lord when l get to heaven please give me an opportunity to meet my sisters who served you with such passion. The Lord heard my prayer and six months later we met at the South East Prayer Leaders conference in Ashburnham Place.

A bride without spot

Printed in Great Britain
by Amazon